## When Christians Disagree
Series Editor: Oliver R. Barclay

*Politics and the Parties*
Editor: Jonathan Chaplin

**Also in this series**

*The Role of Women*
Editor: Shirley Lees

**In preparation**

*The Church and its Unity*
Editor: Alan F. Gibson

When Christians Disagree

# Politics and the Parties

Editor: Jonathan Chaplin

Francis Bridger
Pete Broadbent
Sir Fred Catherwood
Philip Giddings
Brian Griffiths
Paul Marshall
Donald Shell
Alan Storkey

**Inter-Varsity Press**

INTER-VARSITY PRESS
*38 De Montfort Street, Leicester LE1 7GP, England*

*First published 1992*

**British Library Cataloguing in Publication Data**
A catalogue record for this book is available from the British
Library.

ISBN 0-85110-960-8

Set in Linotron Melior

Photoset in Great Britain by Parker Typesetting Service,
Leicester
Printed in Great Britain by
Cox & Wyman Ltd, Reading, Berkshire

*Inter-Varsity Press is the book-publishing division of the
Universities and Colleges Christian Fellowship (formerly the
Inter-Varsity Fellowship), a student movement linking Christian
Unions in universities and colleges throughout the United
Kingdom and the Republic of Ireland, and a member movement
of the International Fellowship of Evangelical Students. For
information about local and national activities write to UCCF,
38 De Montfort Street, Leicester LE1 7GP.*

# Contents

## Part 3 Views from outside:
## Independent assessments of the main parties

# When Christians Disagree

## Introducing the series

There are many subjects on which the teaching of the Bible is quite clear. There is a substantial core of Christian theology and ethics that we can confidently proclaim as 'biblical teaching', and those rejecting as well as those accepting the authority of that teaching will agree that such a core exists.

As we try to work out the application of biblical teaching in detail, however, we find areas in which there is no such clear consensus. Christians who are trying equally to be obedient to the teaching of Christ and his carefully instructed apostles come to different conclusions about such subjects as baptism and church government. Some of their differences have been resolved after debate. In Protestant circles, for instance, few would now wish, as some once did, to excommunicate people for advocating birth control. Further discussion has brought substantial agreement. Some questions, however, are not so easily resolved at present; and there is a need for healthy discussion among Christians so that we may arrive, if possible, at an agreed view. If that is not possible, then all of us need to re-examine our view in the light of Scripture and to exchange views, so that we may ensure that our position is not the product of wishful thinking, but is really faithful to the Bible. All of us are influenced in our thinking by our traditions, our education and the general climate of thought of our age. These forces tend to mould our ideas more than we realize, and to make us conform to the fashion of our time, or the traditions in which we were brought up, rather than to revealed truth.

This series of books under the title of *When Christians Disagree* attempts to tackle some of these current debates. Each book has the same fundamental structures. A series of starting 'theses', or a statement of a position (usually excluding the more extreme views on either side), has been sent to the writers. They have been asked to agree or disagree with the 'theses' and to set out a Christian position as they see it. They then have the opportunity to respond to one or more of the other articles written from a different point of view from their own. A short closing summary attempts to clarify the main issues in debate.

All the contributors seek to be ruled by Scripture. Since they do not agree between themselves, the crucial issue is whether one view or another is more consistent with the teaching of the Bible. Some of the problems arise out of the impact upon us of new cultural patterns. These new patterns may or may not be healthy, and that has to be judged by the application of biblical truth which is always health-giving – the good and acceptable and perfect will of God. We are not arguing whether it is easier to believe or do one thing or another in today's world. We are not even asking whether a Christian position seems stupid to the cultured person of today. We are asking whether there are revealed principles that give us at least some guidelines, and perhaps even a clear answer to our problems.

The Bible is authoritative in more than one way: in some areas explicit teaching is given; in other areas the question is left open in such a way that we know there is no universal 'right' answer. Worship provides an example. There are some broad principles; but the Bible seems authoritatively to allow, and perhaps implicitly to encourage, variety in the details of the style and ordering of worship. In such cases we will solve the problem in our own age and culture in obedience to the more basic explicit teachings that we have.

In the areas that this series explores there are some things laid down clearly in Scripture and some that are not. There is, for instance, no biblical instruction as to whether husband or wife should dig the garden; there are no explicit limits drawn to the coercive powers of the state, nor any delineation of the nature of the world before the fall – except that it was very good.

The arguments, therefore, concern first of all whether the Bible does or does not settle certain questions and secondly how far we can go in confident application of those biblical truths that we are given. The demarcation line between these here is important. If we can agree what is clearly taught then all else is in a secondary category, where we know that human opinion is fallible. Some of our discussion is above the line and is therefore most important. Some falls below it and cannot be as vital, even if in practical terms we have to adopt a policy.

*Oliver R. Barclay*

# Introduction

The purpose of this book is to contribute to the continuing debate about the standpoints of the main British political parties – their compatability with some central political implications of Christian faith. It is the first published attempt by Christians to engage in such a party political debate on the basis of specific biblical themes. A decade or so ago the suggestion would have been regarded by many as either inherently unfeasible, dangerously divisive, or even faintly indecent. The following chapters demonstrate that party political debate amongst Christians need be none of these things. In modern democracies national politics is necessarily party politics. If Christian participation in the political arena is to be effective it must proceed on the basis of an informed and critical understanding of the parties which dominate this arena. If this book assists those seeking such an understanding it will have gone some way towards achieving its purpose.

The book follows the basic pattern of the other books in the series 'When Christians Disagree', though with some modifications. Authors are divided into three groups, each tackling different aspects of the problem in the light of a set of opening theses. (These follow this Introduction.) The two authors in the first part address, from contrasting angles, the general question of whether a distinctive Christian political standpoint is in principle possible. In the second part, representatives of the three main British parties are invited to evaluate their party in Christian terms. The two authors in the third part offer independent and contrasting Christian assessments of

British parties. A specific question is addressed to the authors within each part, inviting them to comment on the opening theses from a particular angle. Each author then replies to the other author or authors in the same group.

The purpose of the opening theses is not to present a particular viewpoint but, first, to indicate some broad biblical and theological themes relevant to a Christian view of politics, and second, to suggest possible general implications of these themes for today. Theses 1–6 summarize some general principles regarding the nature and purpose of politics and the state, and Christian involvement within them. Authors are assumed to be in broad agreement with these principles and they are included here simply to indicate what the debate is *not* about.

Debate is intended to focus on issues arising from theses 7–19. These issues relate to the question of the role of the state in economic and welfare policy. It is not suggested that these are the only, or even necessarily the most important, areas in which political parties differ today. They are, however, central and recurring matters in contemporary party political debate. Theses 7–12 highlight some main features of biblical teaching relevant to this theme, while theses 13–19 list some possible implications of such teaching for contemporary economic and welfare policy.

Adopting this scheme as a way to confine debate has of course meant excluding other important areas in terms of which British political parties also need to be assessed, such as 'life' issues, gender, education, civil rights, foreign and defence policy. The book is further limited in scope in lacking representatives of either the nationalist parties (though these tend not to be distinctive in terms of economic or welfare policies), or the Green Party (though some authors do explicitly address ecological concerns).

Finally, a word on the 'Appendix'. Several authors critically discuss what has come to be termed 'Thatcherism', but no author was available at the right time to defend it. Since Sir Fred Catherwood's contribution is (as he would acknowledge) hardly an apology for Thatcherism, it was felt desirable to complement it by including the article by Brian (now Lord) Griffiths, who was closely involved with the development of Mrs Thatcher's policies as head of her Policy Unit in 10 Downing Street. The article was originally composed for a different purpose, but it lucidly addresses several themes central to this book (as the book's conclusion points out). I am grateful to Hodder and Stoughton, its publisher, and to Lord Griffiths, for permission to reproduce the article here.

*Jonathan Chaplin*

# Opening theses

It is assumed that contributors broadly agree with theses 1–6, which summarize some general Christian principles regarding the nature and purpose of politics and the state, and Christian involvement within them.

1. It is God's will that there should be a political order within human society. Whether viewed as based in creation, or given as a result of the fall, political authority is granted and limited by God for the benefit of human beings. It is responsible for promoting, in the public realm, righteousness, justice and peace and for restraining and punishing evil (Jdg. 2:16; Pr. 8:15–16; Jn. 19:11; Acts 19:35–40; Rom. 12:18 – 13:7; 1 Tim. 2:1–2; 1 Pet. 2:13–14). It should do this today through the establishment and enforcement of a public framework of laws, regulations and conditions which reflect its God-given mandate. All of these must be directed by what is right and not merely by public opinion (Mt. 27:24), the electoral self-interest of parties, or the vested interests of particular groups. It must always act fairly and impartially (Dt. 16:18–20; 2 Ch. 19:5–7; Pr. 29:14).

2. Although no single form of government is given by God, Christians today should be committed to supporting and strengthening lawful, constitutional and responsible government (Dt. 17:14–20), and representative, democratic institutions (Nu. 1:16; 26:9; 2 Sa. 5:3). The state should respect those civil rights which protect the basic dignity and liberty of responsible human beings made in

the image of God, such as the rights to life, to not be harmed, to religious liberty, to freedom of speech and movement, to join or not to join an association, to peaceful assembly.

3. Christians are called to live righteously, justly and peaceably in all realms of their lives (Dt. 5:16–20; Ezk. 18:5–9; Rom. 13:7–8; 1 Pet. 1:14–16). By so doing they help make the task of the state less burdensome. One realm of Christian discipleship today is the responsible exercise of the rights and duties of citizenship (Rom. 13:5–7) such as voting, respecting the law, paying taxes, contributing to public debate, calling the state to fulfil its proper task, and attempting to change its policies when it fails in this task. Some Christians are called to participate more actively through political organizations or parties, or by seeking and exercising political office. As in all realms of life, this necessarily requires that Christians co-operate, critically and humbly, with non-Christians.

4. One task of the church is to equip Christians, through biblical teaching and training, to engage in responsible citizenship. Its official representatives may at times make public statements on important moral issues (and some Christians also accept that such statements may have political ramifications), but the primary responsibility for making the Christian voice heard in politics lies with Christian citizens and Christian politicians. Though accepting the authority of government, Christians must bring to bear a biblically-informed mind on government or party policies, while recognizing that a wholly Christian organization of society will never be attained in the present age. Though given for our good, governments frequently act sinfully (1 Sa. 8:3; Acts 25:10–12; Rev. 13:4,7), and no Christian can give unqualified allegiance to any government (Dn. 3:18; Lk. 1:52; 20:25; Acts 5:29), or the principles or policies of any political party.

5. The function of political parties is primarily to advocate and seek to implement a coherent set of political convictions. They may agree on certain particular issues but the disagreements between them are genuine and

systematic; that is, they reflect different underlying conceptions of what constitutes a good and just society. A degree of Christian influence can be seen in the shaping of each of these conceptions, but the influence of secular thought is also clearly visible. Today, many of the most pronounced disagreements between parties arise over the role of the state in economic life and welfare provision. Christians voting for, or joining, a party are thus expressing a preference for (among other things) that party's view of the role of the state in these areas. Such preferences ought to be guided by Christian principles reflecting biblical teaching.

6. Although there can be no immediate implementation of particular regulations or prescriptions contained in the Bible, its overall ethical teaching does reveal something of God's enduring will for the ordering of human society, and in this sense must be regarded as a normative guide for Christians today. The ethical teaching of the New Testament is a fulfilment and deepening of, rather than an abrogation of, the ethical teaching of the Old Testament.


Theses 7–19 summarize points which are intended to be the focus of the debate. Theses 7–12 highlight some main features of biblical ethical teaching relevant to the question of the role of the state in economic life and welfare provision. One important area of debate is likely to focus on whether contributors think they accurately express such teaching.

7. The economic potentials of creation are a gift from God (Dt. 8:6–10; 2 Cor. 9:7–9; 1 Tim. 4:4). Trust in God's provision liberates people from economic anxiety (Mt. 6:30–33). The cultivation of such economic potentials is one of the ways in which human beings are to respond to the original mandate to develop culture given in Genesis 1:28–9. The fruits of the earth and the natural multiplication of flocks and herds are seen as a proper result of economic activity, and the resulting abundance is often

depicted as a divine blessing on obedience (Dt. 7:12–13). Buying and selling are assumed to be a normal and acceptable feature of economic life, though they were subject to norms such as fairness and justice (Lv. 19:35–6; Mi. 6:11). The freedom to engage in economic activity is assumed to be essential to a full human life.

8. Productive and meaningful work is God's gift to all human beings (Gn. 2:15; Ec. 5:18). Work is a responsibility for all who are able and idleness is condemned (2 Thes. 3:10–12), though rest is essential (Dt. 5:12–15). Those employed by others have a right to a just wage (Jas. 5:4).

9. Production, distribution and consumption are to be carried out under divinely given norms. Goods and services must be produced with stewardship, distributed in justice and consumed in moderation. Stewardly production involves avoidance of waste and permanent damage to the environment (Ex. 23:10–13; Dt. 22:6–7). Moderate consumption means avoiding excessive luxury, restraining acquisitiveness and being willing to share surpluses with those in need (Dt. 8:12–18; 1 Tim. 6:6–10; Acts 2:44–45; Mt. 6:19; Lk. 3:10–14).

10. Just distribution requires at least that every person has access to those basic resources needed for physical life, security, health and social dignity. The Old Testament principle of the inalienability of family land tenure (Dt. 19:14; 1 Ki. 21:3) ensured that every family had a legal right to sufficient productive resources to live on. There are strong denunciations of those who deprived people of this right (Is. 10:1–2; Mi. 2:1–2; Mt. 21:12–13; Mk. 12:40). People have a right to their own property and possessions (Dt. 5:19; Eph. 4:28), subject to the requirements of social justice. Each family ought to enjoy a condition of economic independence (1 Ki. 4:25; Mi. 4:4). In the New Testament, Christians are expected to follow Jesus' example in being willing to forego their rights in order to serve others (Mt. 5:38–48; Mk. 12:41–44; Lk. 6:32–36).

11. A variety of legal and other provisions existed in the Old Testament which were intended to restore those who had fallen into poverty to a position of economic independence and social dignity (Ex. 22:21–27; Lv.

19:9–15; Dt. 15:1–18; Ru. 4:9–10; Mt. 6:12; Lk. 4:18–19; 19:8–9; 2 Cor. 8:14–15). Everyone was commanded to help the poor (Is. 1:17; Mt. 25:35–40), but the king especially was required to defend their rights (Ps. 72:1–4). If all these provisions were fulfilled, no family would be permanently bound in poverty. Such provisions did not necessarily guarantee that everyone would possess equal wealth or earn equal income. It was recognized that a state of poverty could weaken resistance to sin (Pr. 30:8–9) and that economic oppression could deafen people to the word of God (Ex. 6:9).

12. The authority of political rulers is to be carefully limited to their proper rights and duties (1 Sa. 10:25; Dt. 17:14–20; Rom. 13:3–4). Authority, in the perspective of the kingdom of God, is seen as service to human beings (Mt. 20:25–28). Political leaders are not to take to themselves responsibilities given by God to others (2 Ch. 26:18). Political power in Old Testament Israel was initially widely dispersed throughout the nation (Dt. 16:18). Kings were not to accumulate excessive wealth for their private use (Dt. 17:16–17), and rebuked when they arbitrarily seized the rightful property of others (1 Ki. 21). The denial of economic freedom was one of the signs of the demonic state depicted in Revelation (13:16–17).

Theses 13–19 list some possible implications of theses 7–12 for our contemporary understanding of the role of the state in economic life and welfare provision. A further important area of disagreement in the debate is likely to focus on whether contributors think that these are indeed legitimate implications, and what their concrete application might involve.

13. The overall task of the state in economic life and welfare provision is to enable and encourage each person, family, community or institution to fulfil its particular responsibilities within society, and to satisfy the legitimate rights of each.

14. Every household has the primary responsibility for

earning its own living where possible and the right to sufficient employment opportunities to make this possible. The state pre-eminently, but also businesses, trade unions and financial institutions, have responsibilities to help create conditions in which this state of affairs exists.

15. The state is responsible for ensuring that those unable to provide for their own needs, for whatever reason, should be supported, if necessary through direct provision. The state has the right to tax economic institutions and those in paid employment in order to fulfil this and other necessary duties. State welfare provisions should aim at restoring people to economic independence where possible and should be administered with due respect for personal and social dignity.

16. Increasing economic growth and reducing economic inequalities are legitimate goals for the state, but must not be pursued at the expense of the state's general responsibilities to secure justice, righteousness, peace and stewardship.

17. Business corporations exist to produce needed goods and services. In doing so they ought to respect the environment and allow rewarding work and meaningful participation for employees. Although they may earn sufficient profit to enable them to do these things, maximizing their profits or sales or size ought not to be their principal goals. The state has a duty to safeguard the freedom of businesses to fulfil their proper purposes and to ensure that they remain within them, by means of legislation, taxation, subsidy, regulation or advice. Financial institutions exist to serve businesses and persons in their legitimate economic tasks and the state may similarly protect and regulate them to this end.

18. Trade unions exist to protect the economic and social rights of their members and they may engage in collective action and, if necessary, industrial action to do so. But they must also be concerned with the economic and social welfare of wider society and with the rights of individuals. They also share the responsibility with the state and other economic institutions to promote stewardly production, just distribution and moderate

consumption. The state has a duty to safeguard their freedom to fulfil their legitimate tasks, and to ensure that they remain within them, by legislation or other means.

19. Consumers have a right to expect sufficient amounts of needed goods and services and a responsibility not to become acquisitive, envious or wasteful, nor to demand from economic institutions or from the state more than can be supplied without breaking the norms of justice and stewardship.

# The questions addressed in each part

**Part 1: Is a Christian political standpoint possible?**
*Donald Shell and Paul Marshall*
Can a coherent and distinctive Christian understanding of the role of the state in economic life and welfare provision be developed from the principles expressed in theses 7–19 (or those plus others you consider to be of central relevance)? Such Christian understanding is one which could be distinguished from, and be as comprehensive in its implications as, that found in Conservatism, liberalism or socialism.

**Part 2: Christianity and the parties**
*Pete Broadbent, Francis Bridger and*
*Sir Fred Catherwood*
To what extent does your party's view of the role of the state in economic life and welfare provision reflect biblical principles? Are they contained in theses 7–19 (and any additional ones you consider to be of central importance), and why do you think your party reflects such biblical principles more fully than the other main parties?

**Part 3: Views from outside**
*Alan Storkey and Philip Giddings*
To what extent do you think that the views of the role of the state in economic life and welfare provision held by each of the main parties reflect the biblical principles contained in theses 7–19 (and any additional ones you consider to be of central relevance)? What implications would you draw from your conclusions regarding Christian participation in these parties?

# Part 1

---

# Is a Christian political standpoint possible?

*Donald Shell and Paul Marshall*

Can a coherent and distinctive Christian
understanding of the role of the state in
economic life and welfare provision be
developed from the principles expressed
in theses 7–19 (or those plus others you
consider to be of central relevance)? Such
a Christian understanding is one which
could be distinguished from and be as
comprehensive in its implications as that
found in Conservatism, liberalism or
socialism.

# The shaping of a Christian's approach to politics

*Donald Shell*

Theses 13–19 – on deriving economic and welfare policy ● Difficulties ● The complexities of deriving policies ● Theses 1–12 – can a broad framework be drawn up from biblical teaching? ● Thesis 7 ● Thesis 8 ● Thesis 9 ● Thesis 10 ● Approaching the Bible

A significant change has taken place in the prevailing attitudes among evangelical Christians towards the political process over the last twenty or so years. A generation ago it was much more common than now to meet folk who felt that the pathway of Christian discipleship required them to eschew politics as far as was humanly possible. Few evangelicals became directly involved in politics, and the whole subject tended to receive little serious discussion. Today all this has changed. The responsibility of the Christian to exercise his or her vote in a thoughtful and prayerful way is regularly stressed. Direct involvement, whether through political parties or pressure groups, is also much more widespread. And a great deal more is being written about the form and direction Christian activity in politics should take.

It is doubtful, however, whether this growing readiness to engage in politics has been accompanied by any developing consensus among Christians about the policy direction such political involvement should take. And the example of the USA shows how heightened political activity among Christians can be accompanied by increasing intensity of disagreement. Jerry Falwell's Moral Majority and Jim Wallis's Sojourners are very far apart, yet both claim to be conscience bound to the Scriptures. While such influential yet sharply divergent groups are unlikely to be replicated in the very different conditions this side of the Atlantic, we nevertheless do well to explore carefully the nature of political disagreement among Christians, to see if it is possible to reach a more unified Christian mind, and, if not, to define as precisely as possible the nature of our disagreement.

To assist in this exercise the editor of this volume has provided a set of theses which purport to summarize relevant biblical teaching, and indicate where and how this might receive application in our contemporary politics. This is a valuable exercise, and the theses taken as a whole provide a pithy summary of some biblical teaching, and will no doubt stimulate discussion about possible policy. The question posed for this chapter involves considering whether or not it is possible to derive from the Bible (via these theses or, perhaps, otherwise) a distinctively Christian view of the role of the state in economic life and welfare provision, and one that is 'as comprehensive in its implications as that found in Conservatism, liberalism, or socialism'.

# Theses 13–19 – on deriving economic and welfare policy

Perhaps it is as well to begin by focusing quite narrowly on the question as it is put by the editor. This involves looking in particular at the last group of theses (13–19) because it is these which take us closest to the question of application or actual policy commitments. In doing this it will be necessary to say something about the relationship – in politics generally – between doctrinal principle and policy practice. After doing this we will return to the earlier theses and discuss how valid these are as summaries of relevant biblical teaching for the area of state economic and social involvement.

As the editor has already said, theses 13–19 list some possible implications of theses 7–12 for our contemporary understanding of the role of the state in economic life and welfare provision. Contributors are asked to comment on the legitimacy of these statements as implications of the earlier theses, and also to indicate what they think the concrete application of these theses might involve. The editor clearly anticipates disagreement among contributors in answering these questions. Three general points need to be made about this aspect of the exercise.

## Difficulties

First, it is worth noting the amount of space devoted to statements not directed at the state, but at other bodies, such as financial institutions, trade unions, even 'consumers'. That Scripture must be applied to such groups is not in doubt. Nor is it open to dispute that their actions are highly pertinent to political life. But what we must be careful to avoid is the implication that the state can somehow transfer its responsibilities to other bodies. No doubt the task of the state can be made less burdensome in so far as people live righteously, justly and peaceably (as thesis 3 declares), but a distinguishing feature of the state is that it must correct and punish certain forms of wrong behaviour. The state cannot rely on operating in an environment where other institutions do behave according to whatever biblical norms appear relevant. The theses acknowledge as much in saying the state must both safeguard the freedom of business and trade unions to carry out their legitimate tasks, and ensure that these institutions don't go beyond such tasks. But the implications of this are not followed through sufficiently. What if trade unions – or business – are institutions with a constant strong inherent tendency to extend their activities beyond their legitimate roles? It is all very well to say (in thesis 19) that consumers have a responsibility not to become acquisitive, envious or wasteful, but what if the natural condition of mankind is to be acquisitive, envious and wasteful? If so, then this becomes a part of the context within which the state must function. And, if such a diagnosis of mankind is fundamentally correct, it would be much more relevant to talk about how the state responds to these features of human nature, than simply to pronounce that humans ought to be different.

My second general point is that theses 13–19, as they stand, provide slender guidance for the formulation of the kind of specific policies such as need to be embodied in a political party's programme of policies. They are full of qualifying clauses, undefined phrases and the language of compromise. Anyone with a taste for political argument knows that such a phrase as 'where possible' (see theses 14 and 15) is highly elastic. And who is to define the 'legitimate rights' spoken of in thesis 13 or the meaning of 'due respect for personal and social dignity' in thesis 15? When it comes to the formulation of policies derived from these theses, sharply differing views may quite reasonably be taken. For example, some would argue that thesis 14 pointed directly and unambiguously to the need for a government incomes policy (as an intrinsic part of the state's responsibility to create conditions where every household has employment opportunities). Others would argue that such policies have been shown in the past to have no beneficial effect in maintaining employment, and may well have damaged long-term employment prospects.

My third general point is that I don't think enough recognition is given in this group of theses to how policies are assessed. The assessment of what policy is most appropriate often has much less to do with our understanding of the Bible, or Christian ethics, than it has to do with

our view of what is politically and administratively feas-
ible in a given situation. Government is not primarily a
matter of good intentions; it is about getting things done,
altering outcomes, making some more likely, others less
likely, and so on. Politics, it is often said, is the art of the
possible, and though this can be made a banal excuse for a
timid and defeatist pragmatism, there is nevertheless an
important truth in this dictum which we overlook at our
peril.

## The complexities of deriving policies

The discipline and the practice of politics involves bringing together ideals, values and theories about the just or
good society, along with attention to institutions, rules,
detailed arrangements, existing habits of mind and practice. This is the fascination of the subject – and its great
difficulty. There is a place for dwelling on the ideals, and
indeed for their proclamation. But there is also a place for
the nitty-gritty application of policy, devising proposals
that will actually work in the sense that they will increase
the likelihood of desirable outcomes and reduce the
likelihood of undesirable ones. Between the enunciation
of ideals and the devising of specific policies, there must
be some relationship, but there must also be considerable
tolerance of diversity. Looseness of fit between the two is
to be expected. This is especially true if considered over
time. As public opinion and circumstances change, so
policies once considered appropriate lose their relevance
or effectiveness. There is nothing intrinsically right or
wrong about the great mass of policies. It is usually a
question of their timeliness.

For example, take thesis 18 which deals with the role of
trade unions. What does the concrete application of this
thesis involve? Writing in 1987 one might have given
quite different replies than would have been offered in
1977. In the 1970s union power had grown in an
unhealthy way; union leaders had lost sight of their
responsibilities for the economic and social welfare of the
wider society and the rights of individuals. In 1969 and

again in 1971 successive governments, Labour and Conservative, tried to do something about this by enacting, or attempting to enact, a new legal framework within which unions would operate. Both governments failed, and in so doing served only to enhance the power of the unions they had sought to curb.

Many union leaders, as well as members of the then Labour government, were profoundly unhappy at the 'winter of discontent' and the way industrial unrest ran amok through society. Some members of the newly elected Conservative government again wanted to try and achieve change in one fell swoop in 1979–80, but, as is well known, Jim Prior (then Secretary of State for Employment) fought for a gradual approach. He won, and four successive acts of parliament spread over as many years gradually altered the framework of law within which unions operate. As it turned out that was a sensible approach which has achieved necessary reforms which now appear quite widely accepted. The balance between trade union privilege, the legitimate expectation of society, and individual freedom has probably been struck at about the right point, though perhaps at some point in the future the right to collective industrial action (spoken of in thesis 18) ought to be removed altogether from more groups than is at present the case. The argument is one about protecting the rights of society against groups who might use their particular position within modern society to exert quite inappropriate pressure in support of their pay claims. (This has already happened in the past.) But if the right to industrial action were to be removed it would have to be done on terms which assured the group involved that the rights they were trying to safeguard with industrial action would be protected in other ways. Perhaps the awareness that government may use its power in this way would be sufficient to prevent the abuse that would prompt such action.

Many would argue that the employment and trade union legislation of the 1980s was not responsible for restraint imposed on trade unions, but that it was by 'other means' (referred to at the end of thesis 18) that the

state ensured trade unions remained within their legitimate task; such other means being notably resistance to
public sector strikes, and the toleration of a much higher
level of unemployment than in the past. Certainly the
response of trade unions to the legislation enacted in the
early 1980s has been affected by these factors. And again, I
happen to think that it would have been impossible to
curb the unacceptable face of union power without resis-
ting the National Union of Mineworkers in 1984. It would
have been much nicer to do it some other way, but events
over the previous dozen years indicated no other more
acceptable way was practicable. However, if there is a
time for the vigorous assertion of state power, for polarization and confrontation, there is also a time for concili-
ation, for compromise, for consensus seeking. And, by
1987, the time had come for the latter.

That I acknowledge is a matter of judgment. The biblical
principles involved concern the authority of the state, its
responsibility to ensure justice throughout a society, and
its right to use force where necessary to ensure that. But if
the state is an instrument of God's justice, it is itself also
under his judgment. Governments need authority, but all
too readily they become authoritarian, and start trampling
on the rights of groups and individuals. When do they
cross that line? I would certainly expect Christians to
disagree about that. We approach such problems from
different social vantage points. We are members of different groups to which we owe varying loyalties. Better
that the argument between such groups be in part at least
conducted by Christians who acknowledge the overriding
claims of biblical principle, than that Christians all pull
out of existing parties and attempt to form their own,
which would have great difficulty in reaching agreement,
and in its efforts to do so would have removed Christians
from where the real action was taking place.

Theses 13–19 embody attractive and high sounding
ideas on economics and welfare, but essentially they
simply browse around a number of issues, providing virtually nothing in the way of concrete guidance on policy.
Anyone could develop what is said here to spell out some

detailed implications, for a particular time and place, but the judgments reached would be personal, and very few people, especially among those most aware of the complexities involved, would dare to claim that the detailed policies formulated were somehow more directly or authentically derived from Scripture than those of at least some of their opponents.

If agreement over policies as detailed as those which must be the common currency of party politics cannot be reached, what about the theses enshrining Christian principles? If no manifesto-type document can be drawn up, is it nevertheless still possible to provide some broad framework of principles akin to that provided by, say, 'socialism' or 'Conservatism'?

# Theses 1–12 – can a broad framework be drawn up from biblical teaching?

The first six theses are intended to be foundational. I think the opening statement in thesis 6 is crucial. The Bible does reveal something of God's enduring will for the ordering of human society, and what is revealed must be our normative guide. But the Bible does not, on the whole, contain regulations or prescriptions which can receive direct economic or political implementation in the modern world. Thus the stipulations made in the Old Testament concerning the way Israel was to be politically organized must be examined with care for what they reveal by way of underlying principle. Where principles can be discerned we need to ask how these can receive application in our society today. But this is a good deal more difficult and delicate a task than these earlier theses imply.

The approach adopted, with the constant citation of particular texts, seems to overlook the extent to which a theological task is required if Scripture is to be properly understood and applied. For example, thesis 2 states that Christians should support representative democratic institutions, with citation of three Old Testament texts.

When read these texts can hardly be said to offer the kind of support for modern democracy which is here implied! The thesis goes on to stress the importance of respect for civil rights, and refers to the doctrine of human beings created in the image of God. Now it is surely on the basis of that Christian doctrine that the case for democracy must be established. There is a theological task involved in sharpening the definition of that doctrine so that its applicability to forms of government is made more clear. This is vastly more important than culling odd references from the Old Testament which suggest some kind of elective mechanism may have been at work in ancient Israel.

The whole balance between individualism and collectivism needs to be thought about systematically in relation to the biblical doctrine of mankind. Frequently, the importance of every individual made in God's image has been stressed by Christians. But 'made in God's image' means made in the image of a triune God, and there is a solidarity about the human race, a corporateness, a oneness which also requires emphasis. The Old Testament stress on families, tribes and peoples, is in part a reflection of this. In politics the nub of so many arguments concerns the balance between an individual's rights or freedoms, and the proper legitimate demands of communities. A task of Christian theology ought to be to worry away at this. There seems a tendency in these theses to gloss over this point.

## Thesis 7

Thesis 7, which seems an accurate summary of biblical teaching, points to the acceptance of market conditions within a clear framework of values. But the crucial question for us today is what balance should be struck between regulation by markets, based on individual preferences, and regulation by public power, based on collective decisions about the allocation of goods and services. Again I feel that if Christians are to derive help from the Bible on this question, more attention needs to be given to the theological principles involved, which derive only in part from the application illustrated in the Pentateuch.

## Thesis 8

Thesis 8 speaks of productive and meaningful work as God's gift to all human beings. The way this is stated carries the implication that such work is God's gift to every single human being, but that can hardly be so and in any case it may be a more accurate reflection of biblical teaching – and more 'meaningful' – to speak of such work as being God's gift to mankind collectively. There is then placed upon us the corporate responsibility of seeing that as many of our fellow beings as possible become recipients of this gift. But is work a 'gift' or is it a command? It may be more truthful to say that work is commanded, and that it is part of God's will that this should be productive and meaningful. But the consequences of sin mean that this is by no means always the case. Shouldn't thesis 8 refer to Genesis 3 as well as Genesis 2? There is a sense recognized in Scripture in which work has become labour, often a frustrating, boring, toilsome business from which we long to be freed. Yet such 'work' remains a necessity. If one area which needs more attention is the doctrine of mankind, and the balance within that of individualism and collectivism, another area which demands more theological analysis is the doctrine of the fall. Any attempt to formulate political principles which fails to grapple with the question of evil and its entrenchment in this world, will be superficial and ultimately disastrously misleading.

## Thesis 9

Thesis 9 summarizes some of the scriptural parameters for economic activity. But crucially in relation to politics we must ask what part the state has in ensuring or insisting upon 'moderate consumption', 'just distribution' and so on. The hard questions of politics are not answered in these theses. One could, however, develop the thesis, to say for example that it clearly implies acceptance of the notion of defining poverty in relative rather than absolute terms within any society. Having admitted that, one might move on to say for example that, after tax, income differentials should not exceed a factor of three or seven or ten, but that again moves us on to the area where personal judgment, assessment of administrative and political practicality is once again crucial.

## Thesis 10

Thesis 10 speaks of the distribution of land as crucial to the undergirding of social justice in the Old Testament. Could we develop that into a modern garb? I would have thought reference to the social dividend idea would be appropriate. This, as Bill Jordan has shown,[1] could be developed in practical terms in ways which would appear consistent with the general thinking of both left and right in contemporary western politics. Clearly one cannot think in terms of land in modern conditions.

It could be said of many conflicting policy proposals that they in no way run counter to the teaching of Scripture. The choice between them must be based on criteria other than those found in the Bible. This doesn't mean that the Bible is irrelevant. Far from it. We derive our basic values from the Scriptures, and our fundamental outlook and approach to life should be shaped by the teaching of Scripture. But in devising policies we need to take into account all kinds of other considerations, many of which depend upon the variability of human judgment and understanding.

# Approaching the Bible

The Bible simply does not provide us with the sources from which we could derive an election manifesto for a contemporary political party. To try to do this is like trying to write a modern style biography on the earthly life of Jesus: the material is not available to enable anyone to carry out the task. Any attempt to do so, however honestly, thoughtfully and sensitively undertaken, becomes primarily an exercise of the imagination. But the fact that we cannot write a 'life of Jesus' doesn't mean that the basic principles of his life are not clear. We don't know how he actually ran the carpenter's shop, how he ensured that the business paid its way, how he dealt with quarrelsome or abusive customers, whether he undercut his competitors (putting them out of business?), how hard a bargain he drove when purchasing wood and so on. What we do know is that he was entirely and scrupulously honest, that he didn't act out of envy or greed, that in his life compassion and justice were perfectly united, that he was 'tempted in every way, just as we are – yet was without sin' (Heb. 4:15). And such facts provide the fundamental principles upon which our lives must be based if we would truly be his disciples.

Much the same ought, I believe, to be said of the Christian approach to politics. We have no idea what sort of budget a latter-day Christ would bring in if he were (say) Chancellor of the Exchequer. Would he radically shift taxes on income to taxes on expenditure? Would he dramatically raise taxes on alcohol and tobacco? Would he insist on the abolition of tax relief on mortgages? Would he abolish road fund tax and increase taxes on fuel? – to take a few topical examples. Anyone who pretends to be able to provide clear answers to such questions either fails to understand the kind of revelation given in the Scriptures, or fails to understand the workings of the modern state (or fails on both counts).

The Bible is not a document which formulates principles from which a clear political ideology can be derived by a process of deductive reasoning, still less does it provide definite answers to detailed questions of social or even personal conduct. Rather, the Bible is a record of God's offer of salvation through Jesus Christ, of his dealings with people (individuals and communities) and their response to him. It may be possible to formulate creeds which summarize in propositional form teaching about God, his activity in creation and salvation, but such creeds do not provide precise instruction about how we should behave, nor about the way the church should be structured, or how the sacraments should be administered, nor certainly, about how the state should be organized or what practical responsibilities governments should assume. What we do learn from Scripture is the kind of response God wants from his children, the essentials of Christian character, the values which should guide our decision-making. These are as relevant and pertinent to the Christian involved in politics as to the Christian involved in any other area of human activity. They should shape our approach to the political task, but they do not provide us with material from which can be derived either precise policy proposals or a clear Christian political ideology.

# Towards a Christian view of state and economy

## Paul Marshall

The distinctiveness of Christian politics • Our worldview • Character and faith • Present parties • This essay • Biblical guidelines • Politics • Economics • Understanding our situation • Social analysis • Present trends: the secular pattern • Policy proposals from a Christian perspective • Present policies • Towards stewardship and responsibility • Responsibility for the poor • Government responsibility

## The distinctiveness of Christian politics

My belief is that a coherent and distinctive Christian view of government policy concerning economic life can be developed along the lines of theses 7–19. This I will attempt to show by trying to outline such a view. However, apart from the theses there are at least two other items which need to be considered. One is the question of how we should analyse and understand our present political situation. (I will deal with this matter later.) The other is the general question of what would make any particular type of politics (or anything else) *Christian*. I believe that this problem takes us beyond questions of ethical theses, and it is this matter which I would like to address first.

## Our worldview

I believe that a Christian view of politics is distinct from capitalism, socialism, pragmatism or any of the other 'isms' which affect our political life today. In order to see this we must understand that a Christian view involves more than the application of ethical principles derived from the Bible or from Christian theology. We also need to heed biblical teaching concerning politics itself, the nature of law, justice, freedom, rights and power. The same is true of economics – we must consider the nature of stewardship, calling, work, profit, responsibility and efficiency. In the Bible, judges, kings and stewards have specific responsibilities which are different from the ethical responsibilities of Christians at large.

Our politics also depends on something not directly addressed in the theses – our overall view of God's world – what is now often called a Christian 'worldview'.[1] One of the major components of our worldview is our view of human nature. What leads to genuine human fulfilment? What is the source of human happiness and well-being? In what ways are people equal? How does sin affect our thinking, feeling, acting and wanting? Our answers to these questions have major implications for economic policy (see theses 7, 8, 9). One of the major disagreements between political left and right is not primarily on ethics as such, but on a theoretical and empirical question – how much does human nature change in different circumstances? Usually Conservatives hold that the ineradicability of human sin implies that human greed is relatively constant, and so must be accommodated rather than made the object of fruitless moralizing crusades. They often also view social inequality as due to factors other than inequality of opportunity. Conservatives similarly maintain that human sin will always distort and destroy dreams and hopes of an equal society, and hence that caution, experience and prudence should be the important Christian political watchwords. Finally, they view a powerful state as always an overwhelming temptation to a lust for power and conclude that the greatest care must always be taken to ensure clear and precise limits on state authority and intrusion (thesis 12).

Socialists, or at least Christian Socialists, will acknowledge the elements of truth in each of these claims, but, typically, they will also insist that sin manifests itself in different ways in different circumstances and that, hence, human nature is quite malleable. And, especially as the gospel points to and leads to the defeat of sin, then there is realistic hope for a better and more equal society. In the economic realm, this means that there is the possibility of a society based on mutual care rather than on individual success (theses 10, 17, 18).

These disputes also involve questions about the nature of sin. How does it function in human affairs? How variable is it? How much can it be externally controlled? These questions relate in turn to views of history – where has mankind come from, and where is it going? Are things improving, or are they getting worse? In some areas but not others? What hopes for renewal are there before the return of Christ? What is secularization? Is it a good thing?

The components of our worldview shape, and are in turn shaped by, our understanding of our concrete situation in the world. What problems do we emphasize – sky-rocketing divorce rates and teenage sex? Or poverty-stricken families and teenage unemployment? Our perception of the major trends and patterns in our country will reflect our overall view of the world and also the theories we have adopted.[2] As John Maynard Keynes observed:

> Practical men, who believe themselves to be quite exempt from any intellectual influences, are usually the slaves of some defunct economist. Madmen in authority, who hear voices in

the air, are distilling their frenzy from some
academic scribbler of a few years back.[3]

## Character and faith

Aside from these questions about the Bible, principles,
approaches and theories, there are some other matters not
directly addressed in the theses – matters of character and
judgment. God's law is not some computer program into
which the facts can be fed so that the right answer automatically pops out. Even British law, which in some ways
is fuller, more detailed and more precise than the Bible,
does not automatically provide a clear answer in all circumstances. We still have to decide if an offence did take
place, whether it was of the kind to which the particular
law refers, whether it was a serious example, and whether
there were any extenuating circumstances. In order to
consider all of these we have witnesses, solicitors, barris-
ters and judges. The application of the law is always
worked out by people, and people always need to do some
interpretation and contextualization.

God's word does not always produce immediate
answers, otherwise God would need only calculators and
not human beings. In order to follow God we must be
people equipped and able to apply God's word in many
areas of uncertainty. We must ourselves be shaped by
reading God's word and by continually struggling to follow God's way through the vicissitudes of life. Being a
Christian is not just a matter of holding certain views of
the world; it means being a person shaped by God.

Beyond all these concerns we must remember that
Christianity is not in the first place a matter of being good
people or of having a certain view of the world. A good
moral person is not *per se* a Christian. Being a Christian
means trusting in Jesus Christ. In the same way, Christian
politics is not in the first place 'ethical politics' or 'justice
politics' or 'moral politics'. Christian politics is not agreement with a set of theses. Rather it is a politics which
stems from actual faith in Jesus Christ. It is first of all, faith
that Jesus cares for the oppressed, for us, and for politics;

that Jesus will save the world, including world politics and that faith in Jesus Christ is the key to action in the world, including politics.

These remarks are not intended merely as obligatory pious injunctions. They are crucial to politics itself. This can be illustrated by the Jubilee laws of the Old Testament (Lv. 25; Dt. 15). In the fiftieth year, the time of Jubilee, debts were to be forgiven, slaves set free and land returned to the families to whom God had originally given it. The Jubilee challenges modern notions of property, rights and economics, but it is also more than, and other than, a scheme of economic redistribution. The Jubilee was announced on the Day of Atonement, the day when Israel remembered and commemorated that God had delivered them. The Jubilee was itself a great act of remembrance and a re-enactment of God's dealings with Israel. Its whole structure was that, as God has forgiven their debts (sins) so they were to forgive one another's debts. The Jubilee was built on faith in and gratitude to God. God says, 'As I have done so are you to do.' Jesus expressed all of this when he taught us to pray 'Forgive us our debts, as we also have forgiven our debtors' (Mt. 6:12).

The Jubilee was not just a moral act but was also an act of faith. Israel had to rest and could not plant in the forty-ninth year (a sabbath year) or the fiftieth year (the Jubilee). This was a dangerous thing to contemplate for any agricultural people – no planting for two years! God anticipated Israel's fear: 'You may ask: "What will we eat in the seventh year if we do not plant or harvest our crops?" I will send you such a blessing in the sixth year that the land will yield enough for three years' (Lv. 25:20–21). The Jubilee requires trust in God, a realization that our lives are in God's hands, and that any blessing must come from God.

These examples show that it is no simple matter to relate biblical teaching about politics to the modern world: politics (and economics) are always wrapped up in faith. Christian politics is not only a matter of applying Christian 'principles', but is at heart a willingness to follow and to trust in Jesus Christ as the one who brings political life and is the source of political hope.

## Present parties

If these considerations about what makes a person, a movement, a party or a policy *Christian* are correct, then clearly we should not identify a Christian approach to politics with any of the parties or politics currently on offer. If Mr Jones down the street is kind and upright, we should praise him, but that doesn't make him a Christian. If he cares for the poor we should applaud that, but it doesn't make him a Christian. If he tolerates the foibles of his neighbours, we should admire that, but it doesn't make him a Christian. In the same way we can applaud and support (and condemn) many features of current political parties, but that doesn't make them Christian or their policies Christian. This is why in the end, I think, Christian policies will be different. In order to see this clearly we must consider political policies as more than a set of individual proposals. At the level of agreeing or disagreeing with some legislation on poverty or defence there may be nothing which is obviously Christian. But what is crucial is how these various policies fit together, what patterns of life they encourage, what goals they reach for, what basic commitment lies behind them. One could ask a Christian artist – 'What's so Christian about that brushstroke?' The answer will be – if you're fortunate enough to escape an eyeful of paint – 'Nothing much, you idiot'. But for a Christian artist the flow of those strokes, as the shape of work and life appears, should produce a pattern which reflects the faith in his or her heart. A Christian doctor may also say 'Stop smoking', a command that does not appear to be distinctively Christian, but the practice of a Christian doctor will, I hope, develop approaches and styles particular to the Christian faith.

We may and should support many things in party programmes but, unless a party is committed to giving political expression to faith in Jesus Christ, we can never ultimately feel comfortable with its basic commitment and its view of what will solve human problems. Our attitudes towards existing political parties may be critically supportive but must always have a deeper level of detachment. If we are serious about our faith, then we must have the courage to insist that Jesus Christ alone can be the bringer of justice.

Of course our goal should not be to be distinctive or different. Rather, we should seek to be obedient, to follow the way of the Lord in politics. If such obedience appears distinctive so be it, if not, so be it. Also, our aim is not to develop some blueprint for a Christian society, which we should then try to construct. Instead we should seek to follow the way of the Lord in the decisions and problems which face us each day. If we earnestly do this then I believe a Christian pattern of life and politics can emerge.

## This essay

My purpose now will be to try to lay out some features of a Christian political policy concerning economics. I shall not try to cover all the criteria mentioned above (I couldn't). In particular, I shall not address questions of faith, judgment and character *per se*. These are things which we not so much describe, as hope and pray shape what we do describe. Nor shall I try to cover some of the major components of a Christian worldview. What I shall try to do is outline what I think are some of the major biblical themes concerning politics and economics, describe the present situation and present policies in terms of a biblical social analysis, and finally, give a broad outline of a suggested Christian policy.[4]

One final caution. Any Christian economic policy is an attempt to follow the way of the Lord in politics. It is an attempt made by people and so will always be marked by sin and failure. Being Christian does not mean being perfect or giving the final word. If what follows is not particularly convincing about the need for a specifically Christian approach then we would do well to conclude, not that a Christian approach is wrong-headed or impossible, but that I'm not very good at it. This would be a wise and safe conclusion.

# Biblical guidelines

## Politics

*a. Justice: the task of governments*
In the Bible, the role of governments is always related to
justice and so we first need some idea of what this is. The
sense of justice conveyed by and elaborated in the Scriptures is that there is an order of right relations between
God, persons and things. Patterns of relations which conform to this order are just ones. To deal with someone or
something justly means to give them, or it, their 'due',
their rightful place within God's world.

This understanding of justice immediately raises the
question of what is due to the differing creatures in God's
world. This question must be answered in terms of the
place of everything in God's creation. Everyone in the
world is responsible to God in our particular place. Each
of us has tasks to do and responsibilities to take up. Each
of us has a 'calling' or 'callings' to fulfil. We must be
faithful husbands or wives, loving and wise parents,
industrious and careful workers, caring neighbours,
responsible citizens, steadfast friends. What is due to each
of us is what we need in order to discharge our life's
responsibilities. If we put this in more modern language
we can say that each of us has a right to fulfil the callings
that God has given us (*cf.* theses 3, 8, 13, 14).[5]

Being just requires giving something its right, its created
place in God's world. The doing of such justice is, in the
Bible, related to the task of political authorities. These
authorities are to judge, impartially and without favour,
relations in the creation in terms of justice and injustice.
They are to rectify that which is unjust by restoring things
to their right relation. This restoration implies, and is
itself, a rewarding of those who are just (or on the just side
of the relation) and a punishing (or negative rewarding) of
those who are on the unjust side of the relation (thesis 1).

## b. The limits on government

The mandate given to political authorities is to do justice. But this is not a task given only to political office bearers, for all people are supposed to do justly in all their affairs (*cf.* Ps. 15:1–5; Ezk. 18:5–9; Lk. 1:6; Jas. 5:16). Justice alone is not enough to define the government's role: in order to understand what governments are supposed to do we have to know how a government's mandate to justice is different from that of people at large, in particular which problems are government's responsibility and which are not.

This point is especially important because governments don't have the authority to do just anything that they might feel like. It is vitally important that they be kept in their proper place, for in the Bible there is a repeated refrain concerning the dangers of ever powerful and over-reaching government authority. When the Book of Revelation pictures the coming together of the forces of evil in the world, it does so in terms of a beast portrayed like a political authority (Rev. 13:4, 7). Hence we must be doubly careful to ensure that this particular servant of God remains a servant and does not become a lord or a tyrant. We must know not only what governments are supposed to do but also what they are not supposed to do (thesis 2).

## c. The particular task of government

God gave authority to priests and prophets as well as to elders, judges and kings. Each of these offices manifests a particular form of God-given authority. Each of these has a particular type of service for which they have authority and responsibility from God. God's authority on earth is not centred in any one type of person, or in any one type of institution, be that government or anything else. There are many areas of authority, such as those of husband, wife, parents, employers, bishops and deacons (Eph. 5:21 – 6:9; Col. 3:18 – 4:5; 1 Tim. 3). The laws of Israel also were not all of a juridical, political kind. The basic command to love the Lord your God completely defies any political enforcement whatsoever. It is literally impossible to compel anybody to obey this commandment.

Israel's political authorities were not given the responsibility to enforce all the law. Other authorities have their own place and task.

We are each responsible to God in distinct ways. There is no one body or person on earth who represents all of God's authority. Neither the emperor, nor the apostle, nor the master, nor the teacher, nor the parent, nor the husband or wife, can claim to be the only or the ultimate authority. One of these cannot override another in the other's proper sphere of authority. Each and all have the responsibility, and the authority that goes with it, to do a particular task within the creation (thesis 12).

We can delineate part of government's authority by realizing that it should not override other authorities such as those of the church, the parent, or the individual person. The authority of government ends where the authorities of others begin. In fact we can say more, because, unlike the family or the church, the government is not given any specific zone within the creation where it is to act. Yet, at the same time, government is charged with the responsibility for maintaining an *overall* order of justice. In the light of these two things, taken together, we may say that the governing authority's task is to *justly interrelate the authorities, the areas of responsibility, of others within the creation*. Government is not to supplant other authorities but it is to make sure that relations, such as those between person and person, family and family, church and church, or church and state, are ones which conform to God's requirements for a just order (theses 2, 10, 13, 14, 17, 18).

## Economics

### a. Current approaches

In order to understand what policies governments should follow with respect to economics we need to get a clearer sense of what the Bible says economics is all about. There are two main approaches which Christians use in trying to relate their faith to economics. One approach stresses that

Christianity provides certain goals or guidelines, such as full employment, individual freedom, or fair distribution of goods. Then a particular type of economic analysis or policy, usually borrowed from secular theory, is promoted as a means of achieving these goals. In this approach the actual *content* of economics is taken for granted. The crucial question is what *goal* we are trying to achieve with our economics. Christian faith is limited to setting economic goals. In this approach most of the content of the 'Christian' policy is determined by the type of economic analysis chosen.

The other approach considers various current economic theories – such as Keynesianism, monetarism, central planning, supply side, and so forth – and tries to decide between these theories on the basis of Christian ethics. In this approach Christian faith affects the choice of a pattern of economic thought and analysis. However the choice is still between the given, secular patterns of thought: the nature of economics is still taken for granted.

The Bible, however, does not give only goals or ethics which must then be supplemented by modern secular thought. It says many things about economics itself: not of course in a precise, theoretical way, but by speaking to the basic points out of which any economic theory develops.

### b. Economics and stewardship

The modern word 'economics' is derived from the Greek *oikonomia*, a word usually translated in the Bible as 'stewardship'. Biblically, to be economical is to be a good steward.

A steward is appointed in the master's stead to look after his house and property in the way the master wants, and to give account to the master of what he has done. This is why stewardship is one way of describing the task of mankind on the earth. We are to manage it as good stewards who seek to do our master's will and who will give an accounting of our stewardship on the last day. Jesus used stewards as examples, both good and bad, of how we should understand citizenship in the kingdom of God (*cf*. Lk. 12:35–48; 16:1–13; 19:11–27).

We are stewards not only of natural things like land, soil, trees, oceans and minerals. We are the stewards of *all* things – time, energy, health, organization, family life, work styles, buildings – everything that exists in human life. To steward these things is to treat them in the way that God calls us to treat them, being careful to attend to all the ways in which we can express love – through justice, beauty, preservation, use and faithfulness. To steward something we must be aware of its proper place in God's creation, being sensitive to all the ways it can be hurt, and being knowledgeable of all the ways it can bring benefits to others. We must both preserve it *and* cause it to be 'fruitful' – to care for it so that what is good is preserved and to use it so that it brings blessing to others (thesis 7).

Stewardship can be illustrated through the example of a family. Let us suppose that the husband is offered a new job at higher pay a few hundred miles away. If the family is Christianly responsible then it will get together to talk about what will be lost and what will be gained, for them and for others, by taking or not taking the new job.

On the 'loss' side might be such things as: disruption of the children's schooling and friendships and neighbourhood; separation from a church community; separation from friends and ties; separation from the extended family, grandparents, aunts, uncles and cousins; leaving a known and happy work situation; depriving a work-place of a valuable employee; the physical and emotional disruption of the move itself.

On the 'gain' side may be: more money (not to be sniffed at); more challenging work (thesis 8); work which is of better service; the possibility of joining or helping develop a new church community; moving closer to the extended family; widening circles of friendship, and so on.

The family will weigh the benefits and losses of the proposed move and decide whether overall it is a good thing to do. In trying to make a decision this way they are engaging in the activity the Bible calls stewardship. It is basic economic activity. Real economics is an activity that tries to deal with *everything* in a stewardly way (theses 7, 9).

But we (as companies or, perhaps, as families or churches) don't usually make decisions this way (see theses 16, 17, 18, 19). Companies, for example, look only at a few of the costs and benefits. The benefits emphasized inside the company are income and profits. The costs emphasized internally are payments which must be made for wages, rent, raw materials, cleaning up pollution and borrowing money. Then if these particular benefits are greater than these particular costs, the company proceeds with the project, if it can. But it is quite possible that the benefits the company cares about may be greater than the costs it cares about even though the *overall* costs may be much greater than the benefits. What is good for the company (or family, or church, or individual) may be actually uneconomic. We continually neglect all sorts of costs in our present 'economic' decision-making. Instead of being properly economic (stewardly) in our dealings with all things, we focus only on certain things, usually ones which have a price tag, and make a decision on their basis only. Consequently we can (and often do) end up consistently making decisions that are really uneconomic: decisions that consistently have greater real costs than benefits, decisions that make us poorer as people while we maintain the illusion that we are 'growing' economically. The country can fall apart even while economic indicators look good (see thesis 9).

I have emphasized that a Christian view of anything cannot really be developed or appreciated as *one* item or policy, but must be understood as one part of an *overall approach* to political life. Nevertheless the notion of stewardship seems to be one that has no real equivalent in secular circles. Of course people emphasize that life is more than money. There has also been discussion of the 'environment', ' the limits to growth' and 'quality of life'. Nevertheless these have usually been understood as limits to economics, or as things which need to be considered as well as economics, rather than ways of redefining economics itself. It appears that the notion of wealth as abundance of things, or as increase of choices, still has a major hold on the vision of the secular world, both left and right.

### c. The biblical emphasis on the poor

The poor in the Bible include those who are poor in many ways.[6] The poor are coupled with the hungry, the homeless, the stranger, the widow, the orphan, the sick, the meek, the oppressed, the prisoners, the blind and those who are bowed down (Pss. 10; 146). The command to care for the poor is the command to care for all those who are suffering and sorrowing. We may say that in the Bible the poor are those who lack the social, economic, political, or spiritual resources to fulfil God's calling for their lives.

In the law, God continually commands Israel to care for the fatherless, the widow and the alien (Ex. 22:21–24; Lv. 19:15; Dt. 10:17–18). It was God who brought Israel itself out of bondage and who always defends the poor and needy (Ex. 6:5–7; 20:2; Dt. 5:6; 10:17–18; 26:5–6). The other side of these injunctions is condemnation of those who oppress the poor, including those who do not go to their aid. Amos denounces those 'who oppress the poor, and crush the needy' (Am. 4:1), while Isaiah condemns those who 'deprive the poor of their rights' (Is. 10:2; see also Mk. 12:40). Jesus announced his own ministry in the words of Isaiah 61:1–2:

> 'The Spirit of the Lord is on me,
>   because he has anointed me
>   to preach good news to the poor.
> He has sent me to proclaim freedom for
>     the prisoners
>   and recovery of sight for the blind,
> to release the oppressed,
>   to proclaim the year of the Lord's
>     favour.'
>
> (Lk. 4:18–19)

The laws given to Israel concerning poverty covered both the personal and corporate aspects of their lives. Each Israelite was to be open-hearted and generous to the poor and needy (Dt. 15:7) and there was also a whole series of organized arrangements to remove poverty from the land (Lv. 19:9–10, 25; Dt. 15:1–15; *cf.* thesis 11).

These laws give us a picture in a primitive agricultural setting, of the sort of economic relations that God wishes for people. Their core message is that Israel was to order its whole life together, and in particular its division of resources, in such a way that nobody acquired too much and that those in need would continually be cared for – 'There should be no poor among you' (Dt. 15:4). Deuteronomy adds that 'There will always be poor people in the land' (Dt. 15:11, which Jesus quotes, Mt. 26:11) and so Israel must permanently be 'open-handed towards your brothers and towards the poor and needy' (Dt. 15:11; *cf.* thesis 10, 11, 13, 14).

These laws also focus on God's redemption, for as we have noted, the year of Jubilee was proclaimed on the Day of Atonement. On this day Israel commemorated that they themselves were once poor, oppressed and aliens in the land of Egypt and that the Lord had delivered them. The picture given by these laws is one of redemption, liberation, and atonement expressed in all life, but here especially in economic life. Debts are forgiven, that which had been lost is redeemed, the slate is wiped clean and the poor are to have resources to begin again – we are not stretching the point if we say to be born again – economically (thesis 15).

# Understanding our situation

## Social analysis

The concepts of politics and economics we have developed cannot exist in a vacuum but must relate to our situation right now. Consequently we must understand what that situation is. As part of this, we must analyse the situation. Such analysis is not a neutral or purely scientific exercise which needs to be related to Christian ethics. Rather, our analysis itself must be shaped by our Christian worldview. Here I will try to outline some relevant elements of that worldview.

## a. Life is religion

All action in God's world should be service to God and our neighbours. There is no specific area of life which we can call 'religious' as though other areas of life were 'not religious'. To put it briefly, we may say that 'life is religion', that our religion is what we believe, think, say and do each and every moment of our lives.[7] This means that we should never consider a person, a corporation, a book, or a government as 'non-religious'. Everybody serves somebody. If people do not serve God, then they will serve something else. The 'something else' that people serve are what the Bible calls 'idols'.[8]

## b. Idols

The history of Israel is full of references to 'idols'. Israel's sin is always that it turns away from God and turns to idols. We might even say that idolatry is not just another sin alongside the rest, but is a particular way of speaking about all sin. All sin is an expression of the basic sin of idolatry, of putting something else in the place of God.

An idol is a thing which humans create or find and which they then trust in (Acts 17:29; Rom. 1:25; Heb. 2:18). The worshipping of idols is never a purely formal matter, like having a little shrine in the living room. Such worship is, like all worship (Rom. 12:1; Jas. 1:27), an act of one's life. Idolatry is serving something other than God; it is putting our final trust in anything within the creation. Whatever, apart from God, we hold to be the core or key to our problems is an idol. Just as Habakkuk condemns the workman who 'trusts in his own creation' (Hab. 2:18), so Isaiah condemns 'trust in chariots' (Is. 31:1). A chariot, military power, can be an idol as potent as, or as useless as, Baal, Moloch or Ashtaroth. The worship of money, the act of relying on money for peace or health, is quite simply mammon-worship. And Jesus says 'No-one can serve two masters' (Mt. 6:24).

We should look at the supposedly secular and rational world about us with this understanding of idols in mind. All around us are people and governments believing, trusting deep down in their hearts, putting their lives on the line for the hope that more military power will bring peace, more wealth will bring happiness, more education will bring tolerance, or that the laws of history will bring a new society. All of these beliefs are what the Bible calls idolatry.

It is not that legitimate defence, money, learning, or change are wrong. All things in the creation are given for our good and are to be used rightly (*cf.* thesis 16). None of these, however, can be a cause of hope, a foundation of peace, or a source of love. All of them find their proper place only when approached humbly in reliance upon God's faithfulness, justice and mercy. Further, as the Psalmist says, we become like our idols (Ps. 135:15–18). We create them, but then we, in turn, become transformed into their image. And, as we are the moulders of history and the shapers of society, then we will shape our society into the pattern of the idols, the 'gods' that we worship.

Bob Goudzwaard formulated three basic rules to try to explain the connection between our worship of God or 'gods' and our theoretical and practical pursuits.[9]

- All people serve god(s) with their lives.
- All people are transformed into an image of their god.
- Mankind creates and forms a structure of society in its own image and, hence, into the image of its idols.

### c. Idolatry and creation
With these three basic rules we have the beginning germ of a Christian interpretation of society and societies. While obviously not specific enough for most of the tasks at hand, the rules do provide an orientation, a way of opening up the dynamics of social structures and ways of life. We should combine these rules with our knowledge that the world is not just something that happens to be there, but is something that God made with mankind in mind. As God has created the world good, then the very way this world is made speaks to us of its creator. Even though twisted by and caked in sin, the creation has not lost its character as the expression of God's will. In fact, as Paul says, the creation itself is also God's revelation to us (Rom. 1:18–21; 1 Tim. 4:1–5).

Any Christian social analysis must then seek to understand at least two things – the good things that God has put in the world, which endure and can give healing despite human sin, and the turning of these good things into idols which people worship and which twist and distort that creation, causing destruction and pain.

## Present trends: the secular pattern

### a. *Economics as salvation*

It is not too much to say that in our society a person's worth is thought to be determined by the value of his or her possessions. We seem to believe that the aim of life is to have more TVs, radios, washers, cars. We are bombarded by advertising with the message that material things will make us happy. Our government's overall project is to increase economic growth, which means, quite simply, to have more things (*cf.* thesis 16).

The creed of our society is a confession that peace, security and happiness (all the benefits of salvation) will come about sometime in the future if only we can produce more. As John Kenneth Galbraith has pointed out, 'A rising standard of living has the aspect of a faith in our culture'.[10] It is a faith by which we live – it is our hope for the future. In 1930 Keynes wrote:

> For at least another hundred years we must pretend to ourselves and to everyone that fair is foul and foul is fair; for foul is useful and fair is not. Avarice and usury and precaution must be our gods for a little longer still. For only they can lead us out of the tunnel of economic necessity into daylight.[11]

Keynes' reference to 'gods' was rhetorical, but he spoke more than he knew. We accept avarice and we believe it will save us. We will go beyond necessity and try to reach the realm of freedom through our economic gods. But, as we try to create a society in the image of these gods, they bind us and trap us.

## b. 'Growth'

There is nothing wrong with economic growth (*cf.* theses 9, 16). We should always desire that what is truly economic – that is, stewardly – should continue to grow. Societies are made to grow – to grow in justice, stewardship, care for one another, needed goods, fulfilling work and humane environments. But what we call 'growth' is often anything but truly economic. Our usual indicator of economic growth is the Gross National Product (GNP) which is the gross sum in pounds of all the goods we produce and all the services we provide involving money. It focuses on a particular range of costs and benefits as if they were the only ones or, at least, the only important ones.

I am not advocating 'zero growth', or suggesting that the GNP should not rise. My point is that such a rise, by itself, indicates nothing about human wellbeing. Many things add to our GNP. Smoking and other forms of pollution do, both in consumption and in the medical services which must follow. Marital breakdown and divorce are good for the GNP because people no longer share TVs or beds and need to buy one each. Shift work is good for the GNP, and not bad for marital breakdown either. Eating out is good for the GNP. Eating at home is not. Unpaid voluntary work, such as visiting hospitals or old people does not enter the GNP, but paying social workers to do exactly the same task does. Seeking advice from a friend doesn't help the GNP; seeking the same advice from a psychologist does. The GNP does not record the sum of human economic activities, but only those which are done for money.

Because of the way we collect economic statistics, relevant figures are not available, but it seems to be true that much of our 'economic growth' is not adding new goods and services but merely shifting things away from unpaid, domestic or voluntary activity and into paid activity. This shift itself is, I think, neither right nor wrong, but it is certainly wrong to call it 'growth' without further question. For it can be merely a shifting around of activities, or even represent a breakdown of community and neighbourhood spirit, a weakening of family ties, and the increased commercialization of life. We see all sorts of ill effects – economic costs – springing from our pattern of economic growth. Raw materials and energy reserves are being used up at a rapid rate. There is increasing psychological stress and mental illness, an increase in crime and divorce (which correlates well with economic growth) and general alienation, especially of teenagers. With this growth we have increasing shortages, especially of time but also of opportunities for intimacy and tenderness. Nor, with unemployment, has economic growth in recent years come close to solving our economic problems.

## c. Government 'two-track' policies

Government 'economic' policy is concentrated in that fairly narrow range of economic activities which involve money. Any non-moneyed activities are treated as separate or 'private'. Government's goal is to increase the GNP without too high a cost in inflation. But this process of boosting 'economic' growth ignores many of the real costs and benefits that we outlined earlier. The Welfare State has been an attempt to address these matters, usually under the heading of 'social policy'. We now have government agencies whose job it is to pick up the 'hidden costs', the ignored effects, of our dealing with economic matters.

The combined result is a 'two-track' government approach.[12] One track is 'economic policy', which is to boost 'economic growth' and, if possible, to keep inflation and unemployment in check. The other track is 'social policy' to deal with all the things neglected by the 'economic policy'. The 'economic policy' is supposed to produce enough wealth so that government can afford a decent 'social policy'. Typically, right wing governments call themselves 'realists' and emphasize 'economic' policy by saying that, in the long run, this is the only way to afford the 'social' programmes. Left wing governments emphasize 'social policy' and are often quite fuzzy on 'economic policy'.

The overall pattern is that real economic (stewardly) activities are artificially divided in two. Some costs and benefits are separated out as 'economic', and the others are left as 'social'. Efforts are then made to boost the 'economic' in order to get money to pay for the social. The end result is like a merry-go-round, for as the 'economic' gains increase (if they do increase) so do the 'social' costs, and so the 'economic' must increase even more, and thus the spiral repeats itself.

One aspect of the crisis of the Welfare State is that the 'economic' benefits have not kept pace with the 'social' costs. Governments do not have enough revenue to deal with 'social' needs. These deficits are an indication that for several years our real stewardly costs have been greater than the benefits. Even during times of economic growth in many ways we have been getting poorer and poorer. We produce more commodities yet our social fabric unravels. We have been able to go through the longest period of sustained 'economic growth' in human history and yet have found ourselves in economic difficulties at the end of it. Clearly, we have neglected much real wealth.

# Policy proposals from a Christian perspective

## Present policies

The present responses to the problems, or the demise, of the Welfare State do not get to the roots of our problems. The Tory strategy involves building up more unpaid-for costs, which governments will eventually pay for, or which will work themselves out in the deprivation and suffering of people, families, communities and the environment. Conservatives must be challenged with their own slogan, that 'there is no such thing as a free lunch'. We have to pay for what we use; we have to deal with unmoneyed costs, especially with the real costs and benefits to the poor. But to opt for the status quo or to increase the Welfare State along the lines of the Liberal Democrats or Labour Party does not help us either. Such a policy is a refusal to see that there is a real crisis of costs. While there may be a concern for the poor in these positions they do not face up to the fundamental dislocation of economics in modern society.

Another problem with present policies is that they do not address something which must be at the heart of any Christian social theory, the question of responsibility (theses 8, 9, 13, 17, 18, 19). In general both left and right assume that people will not, and should not be responsible to, care for their neighbours in economic affairs. Both of them tend to locate responsibility only in the state.

Conservatives accept, and rejoice in, an economy motivated by self-interest and the maximization of one's own utilities. The notion that a business has a responsibility, beyond the legal one, to care for its workers, neighbours, and consumers is dismissed as idealistic and inefficient. Problems of the poor, or of the environment are to be dealt with by the market, government, private charity, or not at all.

To a surprising degree the Left shares this analysis. The difference is that lack of care for the neighbour in economic life is not something to be accepted, but rather to be lamented. But the assumption is still that 'private' (i.e. non-state) economic life will be governed by self-interest so that responsibility can only come about via legally enforced limits. When a problem arises, the state is the one looked to to provide solutions.

Another feature of present policies is reluctance to face up to limits – for economic growth, income, or consumption (thesis 9). There are major arguments about equality, freedom, distribution, and wrong priorities. There is, however, a marked reluctance to speak about 'enough' – a house this large is enough, this income is enough, this GNP per capita is enough. While there are arguments over who should have 'more', the end of 'more' is passed over.

## Towards stewardship and responsibility

Rather than debating how much or how little governments can or should spend we need to develop a conception of what a healthy economic life is, and then orient government policy towards promoting such economic life. This means policies aimed at encouraging economic responsibility. Economic agents – companies, workers, savers, consumers – need to tackle problems at their source. We need to assess real costs and benefits, especially to the poor, in our use of time, energy, resources, capital, fulfilling work, and community life and on that basis decide whether or not to proceed with particular economic projects (theses 7, 8, 9). This is a task for companies, and also for churches, communities, families and individuals. In the nature of the case governments cannot *force* someone to be stewardly (although they can make it more rewarding for people to be so). Consequently we must always emphasize internal renewal and commitment in each area of life. We should not assume that economic redirection is solely a matter for governments. Without a real change of heart, we will produce hollow legal frameworks and restrictions which will, in their turn, produce other problems. So economics points out the need for evangelism, including economic evangelism. Christians at work, in unions, in buying and selling, in using things, must begin to move in the direction of stewardship.

We should not accept the two-track distinction of 'economic policy' and 'social policy' for both are essential parts of stewardship. We cannot select either 'realist' economics or 'compassionate' economics. Instead we must avoid the two-track framework altogether and try to make our corporate, family, individual and government decisions stewardly from the word go. We must make decisions about starting factories, developing new technologies, moving families, buying food, and adjusting taxes on the basis of their effect on unemployment, family life, production of genuinely needed things and gentleness to the environment as well as on their effect on incomes, profits and inflation.

## Responsibility for the poor

Because of what the Bible says about responsibility for the poor, we cannot delegate our responsibility. We may not foist our own responsibilities off onto the state and say that welfare programmes will take care of the poor, leaving the rest of us, individually and corporately, to go our own sweet way. We must all respond by constructing pervasive and interwoven patterns in our lives – as persons, families, neighbours, schools, unions, business enterprises and churches – to live in such a way that there are no poor.

A business cannot say it looks after only its shareholders and employees, while the government looks after the needy. The concern of business is to produce in such a way that those in need, including employers and employees, neighbours and consumers, are able to live responsibly and healthily. A family must cherish its elderly and not abandon them to the sometimes not-so-tender ministrations of social workers and old age pensions. A union cannot look only to its members and pass by others in small, low-paying, uneconomic-to-organize sweatshops (theses 17, 18).

## Government responsibility

If I am correct in what I say about the nature of government responsibility and about the nature of a healthy economy then we can say that government has a twofold responsibility with respect to economic life:

1. To develop an advisory, regulatory and legislative framework to encourage social institutions to allow people the resources they need to pursue their life's responsibilities. It is to sanction and encourage businesses and unions to act in such a way that people have access to the goods necessary for them to live properly as image-bearers of God (theses 15, 17, 18).

2. When people are bound in poverty, government must, by its calling to justice, help provide the means and opportunities for economic new birth. Those locked in poverty – the working poor, mothers on welfare, the handicapped, the aged, the unemployed – must be given the opportunities of meaningful work to be able to support themselves and fulfil their life's responsibilities (theses 11, 15).

The government's mandate to do justice requires that it prevents the economic oppression that unstewardly actions invariably produce. Yet, at the same time, because governments are given only a specific task, we must beware of policies that would result in a virtual government take-over of economic life (theses 12, 13, 14). I suggest four directions that governments could follow which might respect both these concerns:

1. As it seems that corporations are unlikely to respond to a wide range of stewardly concerns unless they are held responsible for doing so, they should be structured so as to allow worker, union, consumer and community voting representatives on the board of directors. In this way accountability for all of the effects produced by the corporation can be present at its centre of responsibility. This could become a legal requirement for larger corporations.

2. The tax structure should reflect the amount of costs and benefits that company and other economic activities produce outside of themselves, rather than just reflecting internal accounts, profits and losses. Stewardly behaviour should be rewarded and unstewardly behaviour penalized. This could provide incentives for stewardship and could lead to efficiency, proficiency and the use of entrepreneurial skills in promoting stewardship. In this way genuine economic freedom could channel its energy into a properly economic area of resources.

3. The government's own economic activities must place monetary, fiscal, economic and social policies within an overall framework of stewardship. Items such as money spent on job creation and job retraining should not be regarded as losses but as investments, which is what they are. The consumption of raw materials such as oil or land must not be treated merely as a factor in producing income but as a loss of some of the real capital goods of the country, which they are. We must give account of losses in the natural, as well as the social world so that we do not hold it cheaply.

4. Governments and others, should sponsor economic research which develops economic methods, measures, concepts and policies in the direction of stewardship. We

need to re-understand and redefine terms such as growth, profit, work, cost, benefit, accounting, and then judge our actions in these terms.

These policies will be difficult to achieve, and, even then, they are tentative steps on the way, but they could at least set us off in the right direction, and a step in the right direction is worth much more than many miles in the wrong direction. Nor are these policies ones which are guaranteed to produce wealth in the sense of an increase in the GNP. But real stewardship is, in its very nature, the preservation and creation of wealth in the sense of healthy human and natural life. If our destination is to have 'enough', then we must follow the path of stewardship.

# Response to Donald Shell

## Paul Marshall

I take it that Donald Shell's basic intent is to emphasize the limits on what we can derive unequivocally from the Bible: that it is not a book 'which formulates principles ... [producing by] deductive reasoning a clear political ideology, still less defining answers to detailed questions'. Given these limits we must be humble in our approach to politics and we should never underestimate the pragmatic and historically contingent elements that always play a major part in any political situation or policy.

I agree both with his contentions and his caveats on these matters. However, I seem to differ from him on their significance and on their implications for a specifically Christian approach to politics. Let me, briefly, try to say why.

The limits on the amount of direction which any Christian text, ideology, or principles can give has less to do with the fact that it is a *Christian* orientation than it has to do with the limited nature of texts, ideologies, and principles *per se*. They are only one part of politics. There is also the particularity of any situation. There are also questions of personality, character and judgment. Consequently there is no political orientation that gives univocal policy or 'definite answers to detailed questions'. One may be a Conservative, or socialist, or Liberal Democrat and argue sincerely with other Conservatives, socialists and so forth. Political parties and movements are composed not only of people with a common orientation but also of *the same people* engaged in internal political and ideological struggles.

Even if we consider more precise creeds, such as those of John Maynard Keynes or Friedrich von Hayek, the same diversity reappears. Even Marxism, which is perhaps the most precise current ideology, reveals the same diversity, involving even mutual imprisonment and death.

If we were to conclude from all this (which I don't) that a specifically Christian politics is not possible then we would also have to conclude that a specifically Conservative, or liberal, or Keynesian, or Marxist, or Islamic, or Arab socialist or fascist politics is also impossible, for each suffers from the same diversity and indeterminacy that Donald Shell describes. Hence we should realize that the openness which should attend *Christian* politics should attend *all* politics. Consequently, such openness *conditions* but it does *not rule out* a Christian (or any other) approach.

Political orientations in general should not be thought of as creeds or sets of principles but rather as basic outlooks on life: they give an overall direction. That direction may appear to be vague, or to veer and vary, but through the vicissitudes of life and history we can see a basic pattern emerge that is distinct from others. Indeed, this is how we recognize political orientations in the first place.

Probably the key feature in any political orientation is that about which it is centred. For Conservatives this is something like a reverence for inherited tradition, for liberals something like personal freedom, for socialists something like an equal community. But none of these, important as they are, can be the centre of political (or any other kind of) life for a Christian. We can never take any such single concept as if it could unify our political

63

actions. The unity of our political existence is not found in any particular concept or value in principle, even when it points us to something good. Certainly, there must be a place within a Christian understanding of politics for the concepts of tradition, freedom and equality, but they are not our ultimate allegiances in political action. If they were, it would be a political result of worshipping the creature rather than the creator (Rom. 1:25). Such allegiance must be reserved for Jesus Christ.

Of course we must work out the practical political implications of that allegiance. These implications should cohere around a central political vision which reflects our allegiance. In my essay what I have tried to do is outline some main features of this vision. It views society as an order of justice and rights rooted in creation which calls for a differentiated range of responsibilities (personal, familial, vocational, economic, educational, cultural, religious, political and the like), each of which must be honoured as a specific calling before God. It views government as one of these specific callings, whose purpose is to protect the rights and foster the responsibilities of others to fulfil their own callings.

This vision arises out of a commitment to Jesus Christ in two particular senses. Firstly, because through him God restores the order of creation, and secondly, because all authority has been given to him by God, which means that no human authority, calling, institution, or idea may claim an ultimate significance. Our commitment to Jesus Christ and to his word must be central and must shape and relativize all other commitments.

The distinctive elements of this view may be less immediately apparent in a culture that has had a large Christian influence, but it would become much clearer in Iran or Japan: the 'common sense' of these countries is different from that of Western Europe. In the same way a Trotskyite or a Shi'ite would most assuredly *not* join the pragmatic consensus that Donald Shell senses around the question of trade union power in the UK. His own views are not *prima facie* reasonable to anybody with a markedly different orientation to life. As Christianity exercises less formative power in British culture, Christian differences are becoming much more stark.

Even apart from these questions of direction it is important to note that the Bible gives not only a basic outlook, or ethics, or values, but also speaks to the other features of politics that we have mentioned. It speaks not only of the Ten Commandments but also gives many examples of the practical application of these commandments through the case law of the Pentateuch: the Bible says, and shows, a lot about practicality and particularity. It also speaks of God's gift of discerning the times, which in turn will shape our view of practicality. And even judgment itself is not just some contingent, unconstrained guessing: one can be a good judge or a bad judge. Here sanctification is important: are our minds and hearts schooled and shaped to judge wisely?

Donald Shell's cautions are themselves wise, I think, and they must be heeded. No fully-formed Christian position will drop from the clouds. Christian politics is never just God's word but also includes our all too fallible response to the word. However, this does not mean that a Christian approach is impossible or meaningless. It means that such an approach should be followed humbly and self-critically. But with such humility we need together to heed the words that Paul wrote shortly before his own discussion of politics: 'Do not conform any longer to the pattern of this world, but be transformed by the renewing of your mind. Then you will be able to test and approve what God's will is' (Rom. 12:2). As those committed to Jesus Christ and not to any current ideology, we must not be conformed to the politics or the consensus of this age but live out the uniqueness of the gospel.

# Response to Paul Marshall

## Donald Shell

Paul Marshall believes Christians ought to be able to devise policies which are distinctively Christian, of the same kind of detail as those produced by political parties. On the basis of his essay, however, it is clear that he only has a few vague ideas as to what these should be. And in so far as he – someone who has been privileged to devote much time and thought to the subject over many years – has been able to identify such policies, he acknowledges that they may be wrong, or they may in actual fact be entirely non-distinctive. I would agree with this. For example, at the end of his essay he wants company boards to be more representative; tax policies to reward 'stewardly' behaviour (and penalize its opposite); governments to be more 'stewardly' too and (as a finale) to sponsor research on policies for stewardship!

Such platitudinous conclusions should surely prompt questions about the validity of the exercise upon which he is embarked. My first point by way of response then is to say that those who advocate distinctively Christian policies should reflect with some humility on just how distinctive and how Christian their suggestions really are.

It may be said by way of reply that it is not the policies themselves which are distinctively Christian, but the pattern of policies espoused, just as it is not the particular brush strokes of the artist but the flow of those strokes that produces a pattern which reflects Christian faith. This analogy is I think quite helpful. A Christian artist is unlikely to be recognized as a Christian from any particular painting, but rather from the whole pattern of his or her work, perhaps over many years. So for a Christian politician there may well be nothing about particular policies he or she supports which is specifically and distinctively Christian. But if one examines the life of a Christian politician, if one reads a thorough and fair-minded biography of such a person, then there will probably be a pattern to the life, the policies advocated and the way the activity of politics has been pursued, that enables one to recognize the outworking of Christian faith. And the same point in principle should hold for others, be they doctors, teachers, businessmen or whatever.

It may be said that what is distinctive is less the particular policies than the principles on which they are based, and that it is the latter alone which are to be regarded as normative for the Christian; hence a distinctive Christian political ideology should be formulated. But when this is attempted the themes propounded tend to be very general principles, such as the need for an approach to economic policy based on stewardship, or a need to recognize human weakness and frailty, or indeed a need to recognize human potentiality. While such themes may well embody biblical teaching, they are very general, and the really difficult task is to work out practical policy proposals, especially where there is some real tension between the underlying principles (as with the latter two above). Such general themes are an inadequate basis for a political party. But if the attempt is made to clothe them with enough policy detail to present something that might be credible as a party manifesto, then we come back to the point already made, namely that there is nothing specifically and distinctively Christian about such a policy programme. It may be sensible, decent, honest and wholesome; but then so might half a dozen or more other policy alternatives.

Paul Marshall writes 'if we follow the way of the Lord earnestly ... then I believe a Christian pattern of life and politics can emerge'. If by the latter phrase is meant a pattern of policies as a party is expected to produce them, then I think the appeal to do this 'earnestly' is dangerous. So much time can be spent searching 'earnestly' for the true Christian policies that one never actually does anything. Or someone becomes so convinced that they do have the correct answers (after all they have been so earnest in seeking them) that anyone who disagrees must be 'excommunicated' from the so-called Christian political party.

I would want to argue that the fundamental themes upon which a Christian party might be based are already given expression within the existing political parties in this country. Those parties do draw on a substantial Christian heritage because of the many godly men and women in the past who have served within them. If it is said that that heritage is now being fast eroded, that the biblically based themes are being submerged beneath others hostile to Christian faith, and that for this reason it is now considered timely to form a Christian political party, I would still want to say, better to fight to regain the heritage from within the existing parties than found a new one. Our major parties are reasonably open institutions; they are very susceptible to influence from within. This would be a better strategy than founding a new party supposedly as the guardian of the truth.

Paul Marshall writes that 'unless a party is committed to giving political expression to faith in Jesus Christ, we can never *ultimately* feel comfortable with its basic commitment' (my emphasis). I don't think we should ever feel ultimately comfortable with any political party, whether it claims a commitment to Jesus Christ alone or not, nor for that matter with a Christian school, a Christian publisher or even a church. All these are institutions which remain under the judgment of God. The true life of faith involves working in a committed way within this world of institutions, while very deliberately withholding one's ultimate commitment from any of them. This is a fallen world; the effects of sin are pervasive. However much Christians may cherish their 'Christian' institutions, and seek to sustain them with declarations of faith or a detailed doctrinal basis, they can (and do) still decay and lose their vision. Our only ultimate comfort is in our commitment to a crucified and risen Saviour.

If a Christian political party were established, I still think it likely that it would do more harm than good. Let the declarations of biblical principle be made from the pulpits (wherever these are to be found, such as in churches, broadcasting studios, newspapers). If this task is faithfully carried out by the church it will help to create a climate of public opinion which will make it easier for those politicians who are lovers of justice to fulfil their task.

A question not directly addressed by Paul Marshall, but one that seems very pertinent is: to what extent does he believe that God is at work in the world outside the church (that is, outside the community of believers)? In asking this I am not thinking only of God's work in providentially caring for all he has made; rather I am asking how seriously do we take the doctrine of the sovereignty of God? Do we recognize that he is answering the prayers of Christians by bringing into office rulers and working through governments which in no way acknowledge him? If we do believe that he is at work in such ways (as I certainly do) then living by faith for the Christian in regard to politics surely involves seeking to recognize such actions and to become instrumental in their further fulfilment.

Much of the argument for a Christian political party seems to me to be based on a wish to limit God's activity in the world to Christians. It is almost a wish to keep God boxed up in the church, channelled and controlled by us Christians, written into our manifesto and written out of everyone else's. God may well have gifted others – non-Christians – far more than many of us Christians with intelligence, insight, policy-making skills, and, even though such folk don't acknowledge him, I can humbly thank him for their gifts, and join forces with them in attempting to bring about his will. My political activity in so doing arises as part of my life of faith, but to describe the policies being so pursued as specifically Christian is a nonsense.

I too believe that for a Christian 'life is religion' and that 'to live by faith' is to allow the Lordship of Jesus Christ to guide and shape every part of life. But the distinctiveness that results from living under this truth is not so much a distinctiveness of output (so to speak) but one of input. It is the attitude, the motive, the basic concern to glorify God, which is crucial, not the particular form of policy advocated or even the way such policies are pursued. (Of course, policies which are clearly at variance with biblical principles cannot be followed.) If there is a distinctiveness in terms of output, then I would prefer to say it is one that remains uncashed in any currency that can yet be recognized. If the eschatological dimension is brought into our thinking then we can be encouraged to believe that one day what we now do – groping in the dark – will then be open and clearly understood, visible to all. But it is that day which will declare our work to have truly arisen out of faith, to have been properly Christian, not today or any other day this side of the return of Jesus to reign.

# Part 2

# Christianity and the parties

## Pete Broadbent, Francis Bridger, Sir Fred Catherwood

*To what extent does your party's view of the role of the state in economic life and welfare provision reflect biblical principles? Are they contained in theses 7–19 (and any additional ones you consider to be of central importance) and why do you think your party reflects such biblical principles more fully than the other main parties?*

# A Labour Party view

## Pete Broadbent

Economic activity (thesis 7) • Work (thesis 8) • Consumption (thesis 9) • Justice and rights (thesis 10) • Welfare provision (thesis 11) • Political power (thesis 12) • Some underlying assumptions • God • Humankind • The church and the world • The task for the Christian socialist • Ideology and political philosophy • Classical liberalism • The New Right • Classical Conservatism • The values of socialism

In these days of policy review and rethinking in the Labour Party, a definitive statement of what exactly constitutes current policy is difficult! What follows is an attempt to restate what I would describe as 'Christian socialism' from a biblical perspective, and to relate it to theses 7–19. Where appropriate, I make reference to the Labour Party policy review statement *Meet the Challenge, Make the Change*.[1] The second half of the chapter will argue that the Labour Party view is closer to a biblical understanding of society than that of the other major British political parties.

# Economic activity (thesis 7)

The first, and in many ways the most crucial, question for the socialist is not the existence of economic activity, but the underlying ideology of those who control that activity. Political theory encompasses both ideology[2] and political philosophy. (By ideology I mean a belief about the right way of ordering society and conducting political life, based on an explicit and an implicit philosophy of values and morality.) Political philosophy is the attempt to evaluate the concepts underlying the words and values used in everyday politics. Christian socialists borrow from liberation theology the notion of 'ideological suspicion'.[3] In our interpretation of our own reality, we raise questions and suspicions concerning the governing ideology of that reality, and we apply those suspicions to the whole ideological superstructure. In the case of the economic relationships which we experience, they are not conducted in a value-free framework. Indeed, the rise of the New Right, epitomized by Thatcherism in the UK and 'Reaganomics' in the USA, has more sharply brought into focus the assumptions of the 'free market economy'.[4] Since this is the dominant ideology of our times, a critique is in order.

Firstly, underlying the free market philosophy is a *laissez faire* attitude of possessive individualism,[5] which can be traced through Thomas Hobbes and John Locke, and which finds its classic expression in nineteenth-century liberalism. This philosophy understands the proper motivation of the individual as the pursuit of self-interest. From a Christian perspective, this is a flawed understanding of the nature of humankind, which Scripture depicts as an interdependent and corporate entity both in the church and in the world.[6]

Secondly, the possessive individualism of the free market philosophy leads it to embrace a derivative, atomistic view of society and the state. State control is said to be bad, because it interferes with the freedom of the individual and therefore anything run by a public concern is bound to be inefficient relative to private enterprise.[7] (This is not the case – both private and public sectors contain examples of efficient and inefficient operations.) This atomistic approach also leads the New Right to criticize the so-called 'dependency syndrome', whose origins they attribute to the role of the Welfare State. We shall return to welfare provision, but it needs to be said here that the premise 'each person should have their own dignity and independence' does *not* logically entail the conclusion 'no safety nets shall be provided by the state to ensure that dignity and independence'.[8]

Thirdly, the ideology of the New Right absolutizes freedom of choice, and not only places such freedom before equality in any hierarchy of 'goods', but also argues for the inevitability, and in some cases, the *desirability* of inequality. An argument like that makes the grounds of ideological suspicion well founded! (When those in power argue for inequality, it is difficult to avoid the inference that they do so to protect their own vested interests.) A socialist critique of thesis 7 has to ask the following questions. On whose terms is there freedom to engage in economic activity? Is there equality, both of opportunity to engage, and of outcome? Does the overall distribution of goods between rich and poor reflect God's standards of justice, and how does the economic activity affect the balance of that distribution?

There is nothing basically objectionable about the creation of wealth, but the Christian socialist will want to insist that distribution of that wealth is a proper concern of government (without necessarily prescribing the level of intervention); that the increasing inequalities between rich and poor which the untrammelled market, left to itself, will create, have to be addressed (here the Old Testament Jubilee principle (Lv. 25) has something to teach us); and that the market on its own will not provide the various social goods which are required in society. To illustrate the last point, the AIDS virus, and the social and health provisions required to deal with it, would not be dealt with by the market economy operating in its purest form. In just the same way, the cholera epidemic of the nineteenth century spelt the end of the *laissez faire* liberalism of that time as society grappled with the collective provision required to deal with the disease.

It is arguable that the current Conservative obsession with the market will soon pass, and the facile and mechanistic policies which the Conservative government has pursued since 1979 will be abandoned for a new orthodoxy. In the meantime, we are left with the inherently sub-Christian effects of the dogmatic pursuit of this economic fantasy. These are the vast inequalities between rich and poor; the complete failure of the 'trickle-down' theory (the idea that the poor automatically benefit from the creation of wealth because that wealth will permeate the whole of society); and the selling off of major public utilities, such as water and electricity, without regard for the possibility that the provision of certain goods may need to be publicly accountable and regulated in order to function for the good of all and the health of society.

Christian socialists will want to work for an economy in which the skills of the whole population are recognized and used; what the Labour Party policy review describes as a 'talent-based' economy. Each person's worth and skills will need to be identified, developed, and put to productive use. In an age when the European and world markets are becoming more competitive, Conservative policies have led to a lack of investment in skills, technology and plant. Labour will develop a medium-term industrial strategy which seeks to fill the vacuum left by market forces' non-management. Such a strategy will attempt to address the huge problems of skills mismatch, particularly in our inner cities, and to ensure that a competitive and healthy economy for the 1990s can be developed which will benefit not just those out to make a fast buck, but the whole of our community. As we believe that people are of infinite value, so we will also want to extend their interest in the economy to which they contribute, through social ownership schemes, co-operatives, municipal enterprises and collective share-ownership.

Labour's policy review outlines a threefold strategy to help people achieve independence by building 'pathways out of poverty'. It states: 'Fiscal solutions to poverty amount to so much sticking plaster. Labour's anti-poverty programme must take on the root causes of poverty'. The strategy is based on a statutory minimum wage, a fair taxation system built on the progressive principle, and a redesign of the social security system.[9]

# Work (thesis 8)

Many questions arise here. Does 'work' mean paid work? What does the non-availability of 'productive and meaningful work' signify to those who are unemployed – or, indeed, those who find their work neither productive nor meaningful? If the work that is available is demeaning and dehumanizing, is it still 'a responsibility for all those who are able'? What is a 'just wage', and who determines the level of such a wage?

The Christian socialist will want to ask questions about profits and ownership. Does the worker who contributes to the artefacts he or she creates share in the value created – and is this part of the equation which should be applied when assessing the just wage? Is there scope for profit-sharing, co-operative ownership, or social ownership of the means of production? In assenting to a mixed economy, the Christian socialist does not, and cannot, hold back from criticism of the inherent weaknesses of capitalism as a system for producing creative, fulfilling and unalienated work. Similarly, the distortion of the biblical doctrine of work by the Protestant work ethic,[10] which insisted that work was not only natural to humankind, but also a calling, a sign of election, and an opportunity for thrift and charitable works, will need redressing by an emphasis on the dignity of both work (paid and unpaid) and leisure as reflections of the image of God, an examination of the feasibility of the introduction of the social wage,[11] and a reappraisal, in the context of long-term unemployment, of our habit of assessing a person's value in relation to their job.

# Consumption (thesis 9)

An inherent evil in the working of the free market is its tendency to produce excessive disposable income for the minority, with the attendant obscenity, which was all too visible in the London of the late 1980s, of indulgence, gluttony and waste. Socialism requires the control of personal excess through progressive taxation and redistribution of assets. It also presupposes using both legislation and incentive to enable the rich to share their wealth with those from whom they have profited. Recent Conservative government legislation has destroyed many of the mechanisms for such redistribution. The rating system, which taxed property and assets, was replaced by the poll tax, which had no regard to ability to pay. Labour would introduce a local tax based on income and property values. The Planning Acts, which enabled developers and speculators to make a contribution to the environment and employment of an area out of which they made their profits, have been eroded. Labour would restore the community dimension to town planning. The personal taxation system has had removed from it the higher rates of taxation previously imposed on those with high incomes, in the (empirically unproven) hope that 'incentive' will produce a 'trickle-down' effect within the social structures. Labour will restructure the personal taxation system to benefit the lower-paid.

Christian socialism identifies the danger of allowing human acquisitiveness too much rein, and the need to devise new systems of 'stick and carrot' in order to bring about the principle enunciated to the church in Corinth by St Paul (2 Cor. 8:13–14), which encapsulates the idea of 'from each according to their ability; to each according to their need'.

The global and ecological questions raised by consumption also need addressing. A Christian understanding of both the goodness and fallenness of the created order, and of humankind's responsibility for stewardship of that order, must entail a re-examination of those aspects of our economic system which sit light to the consequences of pollution, the finitude of resources and the impact of policies on future generations.

Governments are strong on platitudes and weak on delivery. Labour policies propose tough environmental regulation, founded on four principles: a presumption against pollution; an insistence that the polluter pays; precaution as the basis for policy; and freedom of environmental information.[12]

Similarly, questions of resources and their distribution cannot ignore the two-thirds world. Overseas Aid, however channelled, has always represented a pitifully miniscule proportion of our Gross National Product. The recommendations of the Brandt Commission Report[13] have been rejected by the proponents of the free market as, variously, too utopian, too generalized, or lacking in evaluation of the comparative worth of the particular cultures of third world countries.[14] Yet these sound like the objections of those who have already decided to do nothing about the plight of the two-thirds world, and to seek justification for their predetermined conclusion that the market place will solve all the problems. John Stott argues that the biblical principles of unity, worked out in distributive justice, and of equality in diversity, are those we should apply to the issue of the two-thirds world.[15] The market provides no mechanism whereby those two principles can be achieved. Indeed, the market, which its proponents claim to be objective, can make no claim to achieve such ends.

It is perhaps worth noting here a delicate sleight of hand which the New Right performs when arguing about the operation of the market. Justice and injustice, it is claimed, can emanate only from deliberate actions; the market is impersonal and incapable of deliberate actions; therefore no justice or injustice can be attributed to the operations of the market. Yet a theology which takes seriously the structural as well as the individual nature of sin, and the insight, born of Reformed theology, that there is no such thing as a neutral or value-free institution in society, must go a stage further and insist that the market can be held to be a cause of injustice, and that, in relation to Britain's economic relationships with the third world, structural injustice is present and empirically verifiable.

# Justice and rights (thesis 10)

Christian socialists would find very little to disagree with here, although the theological grounds for the family as the basic economic unit, based on the Old Testament texts, are inconclusive.[16] Pragmatically, a case can be argued that in western society the family has become the focus of economic independence from other units in society, but we might derive that from a Christian doctrine of marriage and shared possessions, which, in twentieth-century Britain, has become the nuclear family. In other cultures, different economic units prevail.

The implication of thesis 10 is that just distribution must be a major item on the agenda of any UK government, just as it must be on the agenda of the nations of the north in relation to their dealings with the 'south'/two-thirds world.

# Welfare provision (thesis 11)

The issues in the areas of welfare provision have been well explored in the Church of England Board for Social Responsibility report, *Not Just for the Poor*. This detailed six major questions about welfare provision in the UK today:
1. What should be the relationship between the individual, families, neighbours, and the state?
2. What should be the relationship between public and private provision?
3. What should be the relationship between public and voluntary bodies?
4. How much participation should there be?
5. Should benefits be universal or selective?
6. What is the relationship between tax and welfare benefits?

A Christian socialist will want to argue for a mixed provision, with a partnership between family networks, voluntary and public provision, but with the state as primary, though not exclusive, funder and provider.[17] Human beings in the image of God will therefore have access to networks in which their basic economic, health and support needs are met, and where Beveridge's five giants (Ignorance, Idleness, Want, Squalor and Disease) can be fought and defeated. Contrary to popular opinion, they are by no means extinct. Service providers need to be accountable to their users, and this will involve a democratization of the Health Service, more participation in the work of local authorities, and an opening-up of the voluntary sector. Labour's policy review includes commitments to the setting of quality standards in local government, health and education.[18]

Benefits will need to be better targeted, and there can be no real case for the continued separation of tax allowances and benefits. The protestations of the New Right, that the state should not force people to contribute to welfare provision through compulsory redistribution, underline the individualistic nature of their critique. For the New Right, welfare is a dirty word. They allege that it creates dependency on the part of the recipients, infringes the liberty of the citizen to make choices about how to dispose of his or her income and denies the equality of people by allowing the state to decide what is good. Most welfare, it is argued, could best be provided through the private market.[19] The fundamental flaw in this philosophy is anthropological.

It understands the economic human being and his or her choices as an autonomous given. There is no recognition given to the complexity of social relationships in which a human being is reared and exists. Nor is there any ground for believing that one economic human being will treat another economic human being with respect or dignity, except out of utilitarian self-interest. By contrast, thesis 11 recognizes the complex network of Old Testament provision, which was predicated on the idea of community and interdependence. Admittedly, in a theocracy there

were few sanctions (the judgment of Yahweh notwithstanding!) if the basic welfare provisions were not
observed, but the principles enunciated in thesis 11,
together with the biblical themes of equality and justice,
give adequate grounds for the espousal of a comprehensive state welfare system.

# Political power (thesis 12)

The primary questions of power and authority in the state,
and their relationship to the rule of God, are addressed
here; what is not addressed is how the derivative questions of the exercise of political power are to be resolved.
Christian socialists will argue for the appropriateness of
democracy as a mechanism for building in the requisite
checks and balances to ensure that those who wield
power are accountable. In passing, it is important to
repudiate the New Right fallacy that accountability can,
and indeed should, be expressed in financial terms. The
fatuous assertion that the poll tax would make local
government more accountable because people would pay
more 'directly' for local services, was both unsustainable
in theory (because poll tax was unrelated to ability to pay,
and took no proper account of the relative needs of the
communities paying the tax)[20] and in practice (businesses
were taxed on a national basis, and the 'safety nets',
designed to make the tax more palatable when it was first
introduced, blurred into total obscurity the *actual* figure
being levied by a local authority).

Democracy is not, of course, inherently Christian. William Temple argued that democracy rested on an appropriate understanding of the derivative Christian social
principles of social fellowship and freedom, and was,
when viewed from within the Christian social tradition,
the most tried and tested way of expressing those two
principles.[21] A Christian socialist might well want to add
that western liberal democracy, for all its shortcomings,
has produced a situation in which monopoly power is
open to challenge, autocracy is (in theory) prevented, and

government is forced to account to the electorate for its actions. The abuse of Parliament and the process of legislation that has occurred under Thatcherism merely argues for a greater degree of accountability, freedom of information, and a second chamber of Parliament with teeth! Personally, I would favour the abolition of the House of Lords in its present form, and the creation of a body to scrutinize and amend legislation, either directly elected, or nominated on a 'list' system, and related to the relative strengths of the political parties in the House of Commons. The right of bishops and life peers to sit in the House of Lords is indefensible.

Of course, a commitment to democracy being made to work better entails a reform of the electoral system. Some form of proportional representation will need to be introduced, preferably based on the single transferable vote, but incorporating mechanisms to ensure that people retain the ability to relate to a 'constituency' MP or councillor, and that the balance of power is not held by a few members of a minority party, thus rendering the country ungovernable.

# Some underlying assumptions

The unexplored ground in many debates about the Christian foundation for political ideas is our theological understanding of God, humankind, and the church and the world. How do our assumptions in these areas fuel the theology we espouse?

## God

If the God of Scripture is both a God of grace and of unchanging attributes, a God whose future is the ultimate destiny of the universe, then my task as a creature and servant of that God, who has revealed himself in Jesus Christ, is to seek his future, and the change which is required to participate in that future. For this God is a God of paradox: unchanging, and yet with change as his very nature. This causes me to reject the Conservative ideology which venerates and upholds the past and what is – the status quo – because God's kingdom points forward to his future. Equally, I will repudiate the utopian notions of others who have expounded the Christian socialist ideal as the coming of the kingdom of God on earth, for God's kingdom is a rule which is only, in this transitory age, provisional, and merely points to the future perfection of the age to come which Christ's return will one day inaugurate. It is *his* future, *his* kingdom, and it is the task of the Christian community, not to build the kingdom, but to point to signs of the kingdom, and to let it judge and criticize all human institutions with its radical eschatological challenge.

## Humankind

Similarly, with our understanding of humanity, the Christian socialist must avoid the notion of the perfectibility of men and women, and take seriously the cataclysmic effect of the fall. It has been said that Conservative thought, whether of the more patriarchal and traditional kind, or the New Right version, depends heavily on the 'politics of imperfection', undergirded by the doctrine of original sin.[22] Yet in doing so it has arguably been more faithful to Scripture than the utopian strand of Christian socialism, which has emphasized the perfectibility of human nature, and underplayed the doctrine of the fall. As Peter Hinchliff puts it, 'I believe that Christians really choose between capitalism and socialism on their often unconscious understanding of the fallenness of man.'[23] But this is a false dilemma. It is not a matter of choosing between the imperfection of human nature and the perfectibility of human nature and thereby selecting one's political *credo*. If the biblical account of the historic fall which plunged all creation into corruption, and of a redemption achieved through the incarnation, death and resurrection of Jesus Christ is to be taken seriously, we have to do justice to both poles of the doctrine. This means that we have an understanding of the individual as made in the image of God, made in diversity of sex, race and culture, and capable both of startling altruism and infinite folly and cruelty.

Not only will the ordering of society have to take account of humanity's potential for individual and collective tyranny, but also for self-righteousness and insularity. Political reality insists that we remain alert to the sins of Herod and the sins of the Pharisees. Where naive socialism has placed too much trust in the corporate state, and has ignored the potential for corruption and the concentration of absolute power, the countervailing blindness of Conservatism is to the justification of the status quo merely because it *is*, and to hypocrisy, smugness and arbitrary power. The enormities of the New Right are compounded by their ignorance of the social circumstances of the genuine poor in society, and by their total indifference to the evils of that society.

As Ronald Preston argues, 'we need a politics of hope which can take on board all that is negatively relevant in the politics of imperfection, and then go further in the search for creative change.'[24] A pragmatic socialism which takes the biblical revelation seriously will seek to ensure that society is provided with the means so to order itself that human selfishness and human altruism can be cultivated for good, and that no institution or structure is established which is beyond scrutiny and cannot be called to account for its actions.

## The church and the world

When I speak to Christian groups on political involvement, it is often the question of the role of the church which causes the greatest controversy. The current debate between the church and the New Right provides an object lesson in why this should be the case. The New Right's counter-attack on the church has focused on its understanding of the task of the church. The USA provides the paradigm, for it is not the Established Church of high Toryism which is in view. Rather, the New Right seeks to affirm the centrality of Christianity in its own value-structure, but it is a spiritual and otherworldly Christianity, which owes more to the civil religion of the USA than to the Church of England model. Church political involvement is disdained and vilified – the church, it is said, has lost its way and reduced the content of the faith to political slogans. Social involvement should be limited to church concern on 'moral issues', by which is meant abortion, homosexuality and other individual matters.

There are three prongs to this attack: the assertion that the proper concern of the church is the 'spiritual'; the accusation that theological liberalism is at the root of any attempt by the church to undertake political theology; and the definition of the role of the church as guardian of certain specific 'moral' values. (It is arguable that the Polish Communist Party, in its attacks on the role of the Roman Catholic Church during the dispute with Solidarity, deployed similar arguments, depicting the church in this case as a reactionary rather than a liberal force.) The paradigm is clear: the church must be otherworldly, in some way corrupt when judged against current orthodoxy, and must have a defined role which it can be accused of transgressing. In order further to understand the clash between church and New Right, it is worth examining the theological defence of the New Right mounted by Brian Griffiths.

He espouses a Christian moral basis for his social policy which enshrines a particularly individualist theological framework, expressed in the following six 'theses':

1. God reveals his character in justice, and most obviously in the moral law.
2. Individuals, made in the image of God, are created for freedom.
3. The fall is cataclysmic, and there is no redemption through politics, and no possibility of a utopia.
4. We live in two kingdoms, and the kingdom of God is synonymous with the church. It does *not* give us a basis for social ethics.
5. The kingdom of God is no more or less than an example of the life of the church.
6. Creation order is the basis of state order, and is

expressed most cogently in the law of God.[25]

Note that the theological framework which Brian Griffiths espouses first prescribes which theological entry points are to be accorded primary status (God as lawgiver and creator). Secondly, the framework circumscribes the terms in which the faith is to be expressed (individual and spiritual). Thirdly, it seeks to proscribe alternative theological positions (in this case kingdom theology) by tight counter-definition.

What Brian Griffiths has done is to attempt to undermine alternative positions by limiting the terms of the debate to areas which are those within which the New Right has already determined that the church should properly operate; the argument is entirely prejudged.

A counter view of the church might start from the understanding that there is no evidence in the New Testament that church and kingdom of God are coterminous; rather, the church is one sign of a kingdom which expresses the rule of God within the structures of society and within the lives of individuals. As such, there is no need for the church to be impaled on the horns of a false 'spiritual/worldly' dilemma. For the church to express the reality of the kingdom it must always stand over against the world, in 'critical solidarity' with the society in which it finds itself. Where it has a national role, as does the Church of England, it will expect to exercise that critical solidarity in overt ways, and will incur the wrath of the powers that be, whichever government is in power. Where the role is marginal, the church will sometimes be called to the prophetic and costly option of defiance and even martyrdom, as in the former USSR or some Central American states. The proper role of the church will always be to cause discomfort – particularly to those assured of their own rectitude!

The assumptions of Christian socialism are that God is the God of the future, of change and transformation. In Jesus Christ, he has revealed himself as paradigm humanity, and achieved the redemption of the world. Individuals come by faith to participate in his transformation, and find not only their own liberation, but the key to the liberation of society, expressed in the values of the kingdom of God. As members of the church, they work to bring the good news of Jesus Christ to individuals but also to a society whose structures are in need of redemption. The love of Christ and the power of the Spirit motivates them to work with hope and realism for the kingdom which they will only see in perfection when this world is finally transformed into the new heaven and the new earth, which is God's future. In the values of the biblical revelation, they identify certain themes which ring true with the values expressed in socialism – the equality of all people, the demands of a God of justice whose concern is for the poor and oppressed, the solidarity of humankind despite the barriers of prejudice, culture, class, race and gender, and the liberty and true humanity towards which socialism has striven, and which Christians believe is found in relationship with God through Jesus Christ.

# The task for the Christian socialist

## Ideology and political philosophy

Earlier I wrote of the distinction between ideology and political philosophy. This distinction is important for two reasons.

Firstly, it enables the Christian task of analysing political theory by sharpening the questions about the presuppositions and origins of that theory. Here we need to make a distinction between *total* and *particular* ideology.[26] 'Total ideology' is a description of the world-view of a particular culture, society, or historical period. 'Particular ideology' is Karl Mannheim's description of a set of ideas relative to a group's particular interests, and in this definition he followed Karl Marx's understanding of ideology as an agent of deceit. He also understood ideology to be an entirely relativistic concept. The Christian task is to disentangle the various particular ideologies which contribute to socialist thought – liberal humanism, Marxism, socialism, and Christianity – and to evaluate, using the tool of political philosophy, their contribution to the great themes of socialism – liberty, equality, distributive justice, solidarity/fellowship/interdependence and service. The content of these themes, and their credibility as desirable objectives for our society, depend upon the concepts they embody being more than mere slogans. To this I shall return.

Secondly, identification of the ideological content of political theory enables a proper engagement in the debate about values. To understand the relative weight given by the various ideologies to the major political values is to begin to enable the crucial debate that is necessary for the Christian community in this country if it is ever to free itself from its horror of politics.[27]

## Classical liberalism

For the purposes of this chapter, however, let me start with the values of liberalism. It is impossible to understand the New Right without having first come to terms with its roots in what Ronald Preston describes as 'Gladstonian Liberalism'.[28] It is important to see how the New Right has modified the values of the classical liberalism out of which it sprung. Nineteenth-century liberalism is underpinned by an atomistic individualism – human beings are seen as free, rational and self-improving, and the duty of government is to provide the maximum possible freedom for the individual within the framework of law. This means that the liberal view of society is a weak one, in which self-interested individuals exercise their freedom of choice to contract together for the common good. Liberal theorists emphasize the voluntary and consensual nature of society. Equality for the liberal consists in embracing equality of opportunity for all. The individual has his or her own rationality, self-interests and rights before the law – a formal equality which implies that every human being starts from the same basis. Competition, which is assumed to be a given of human existence, will inevitably bring about inequality, as people use their talents to improve themselves. Equality of opportunity is of course not the same as equality *per se*, precisely because it is the base and starting-point from which human beings are able to change and become unequal.

Justice for the liberal thinker is based firmly in the concept of merit – individuals receive their rewards in proportion to their use of inherent talents. Social justice is understood somewhat differently, and can be defined by asking the questions: What rules in society will best govern that society? What is the sort of society that enlightened and rational individuals would choose to live in? This line of thought has been developed most fully by John Rawls in his book *A Theory of Justice*[29] which argues from liberal premises about humanity and society towards what has become a classical contemporary statement of liberal justice theory.

Liberalism owes much to the utilitarianism of the nineteenth century, and this becomes most apparent in its approach to freedom. In weighing the balance between individuals in society, liberalism argues that everyone has equal rights to a freedom which does not conflict with anyone else's basic freedom. Inequalities (both social and economic) are to be so arranged in society that, in theory, anyone is able to attain to the goods they desire by exercising their freedom of choice within a framework of equality of opportunity. Freedom of choice is thus the primary value for the liberal thinker. The individual pursues his or her own self-interest within a rational framework, and, as John Stuart Mill argued, should be afforded freedom of thought, speech and religion as a right which should be curtailed *only* where the exercise of that freedom poses a direct threat to the freedom of others. The individual is also seen as free over against the state. The state and society are entitled to interfere with an individual only in order to protect its members from direct material harm. Freedom is also freedom under law; humans are subordinate to laws to which they have freely consented, and it is within this framework that they are free.

The liberal understanding of interdependence derives from this contractual view of society, and expresses itself thus:

1. Individuals are free agents, and, as such, may arrive at different conclusions from their neighbours.
2. There is no certainty that the truth arrived at by one individual is superior to the truth arrived at by another. Liberalism espouses an empiricist epistemology. We can never know a truth *finally*.
3. To be intolerant of another's opinions is to assume infallibility. It is tolerance which will lead us towards the shared truth of our different positions.
4. This leads the liberal to argue for a pluralist society, in which tolerance becomes a cardinal virtue.
5. Interdependence cannot be taken for granted. All one can assume is that a combination of tolerance and enlightened self-interest will produce a society in which people contract in a harmony of common interests for the good of all.

In a hierarchy of values, the liberal will place freedom at the top, with equality of opportunity the mediating factor for justice, and interdependence defined more specifically in terms of the individual. The chart at the end of the chapter (see p. 95) attempts to depict the relative weighting afforded to these major values by the different strands of political thought.

## The New Right

For the New Right, too, the crucial value is freedom. Liberty is more important than equality, and if pursuit of equality leads to any diminution in liberty, this is to be deprecated.[30] New Right thinking emphasizes the freedom of choice and the optimization of individual self-interest. It has adapted the liberal framework, however, in two very important ways. Firstly, the concept of equality of opportunity is relegated to *comparative* equality of opportunity. It is assumed that individuals in the market place will use their relative powers and self-interest in order to obtain the goods they want. It is the market which is the objective mechanism which ensures the attainment of what is required by the consumer: 'The market is neutral; it will supply what consumers want, from prayer books and communion wine to pornography and hard liquor.'[31]

Secondly, the values of justice and interdependence are played down until they become virtually incidental to the ordering of society. If freedom is freedom to operate within the market place unfettered by the interference of politics and the state, then there can be no question of injustice in the operation of that neutral market. Injustice, as we noted above, can, according to the New Right, only be caused by deliberate or wilful action, whereas the market is impersonal.

Interdependence does not figure on the agenda either. Persons are persons in their own right, and entitled to respect and safeguards for their property and goods. I may recognize my responsibility to my neighbour, but it is an individual responsibility, and I must not be coerced into caring for my neighbour through, for example, being forced to subsidize him or her through taxation or other forms of redistribution. Lord Harris, one of the foremost apologists for the New Right, poses the question 'What is the best way to motivate people in society – fear, love or self-interest?' He continues, 'My argument stands like a tripod on the three legs of politics, economics and ethics '. The choice he presents is one of freedom *versus* coercion. We are asked, on political, economic, and social grounds to accept that the market economy is the best, most efficient, and most moral mechanism whereby self-interest can motivate people for their good.

## Classical Conservatism

Classical Conservatism espouses a different set of values. The backbone of Conservative thought is its understanding of the past and of tradition. What has been, what has survived and what is, have the *de facto* authority of the past. Leadership is best exercised by an elite – though the elite will seek a broad consensus for the policies they wish to pursue (the old 'one nation' Conservatism). There is no assumption that egalitarianism has much to offer, although there is a strong sense of the value of the other individual, and of his or her right to be treated with justice. Indeed, justice in Conservative thought focuses on the individual and one's treatment of that individual.

Conservatism is specifically non-ideological – that is to say, it is suspicious of any attempt to define a particular political theory. There is an explicit statement of the imperfection and the imperfectibility of humanity, for Conservatism is suspicious of utopias, and is essentially a pragmatic creed. Freedom of choice is again top of the hierarchy of values.

## The values of socialism

Socialist thinking clearly reverses the Conservative hierarchy of values. Equality becomes primary – the major political ideal, expressed as unqualified egalitarianism. Justice becomes the means to the egalitarian end – justice to each person according to their needs. The socialist concept of justice is procedural – it describes the correct procedure for arriving at the desired end. Freedom is defined in terms of fulfilment, with the individual achieving that fulfilment only in a context of renewed social relationships, where justice and co-operation ensure the goal of equality.

In the current political climate, there is great scope for an informed debate about these values, and how they are to be achieved in society. Over a decade of Thatcherism has left the country divided, more selfish, with many people richer and many others comparatively poorer. The elevation of 'liberty' defined in individualistic terms over all other 'goods' in society has led justice to be neglected, equality to be scorned and interdependence to be dismissed as weakness. Christians who believe that our country needs to be rescued from the evils which the New Right has foisted on us need to consider carefully which political philosophy and party most closely adheres to those values which will make our society whole and more healthy. The Labour Party does not claim to be Christian; personally I am wary of any political party which plays the 'God' card too frequently. But as a Christian in a democracy, I have to ask, 'Which party most closely espouses the values I believe to be consistent with Scripture?' The answer, as far as I am concerned, is clear. It is the Labour Party.

## A matrix of values

| Liberalism | New Right | Conservatism | Socialism |
|---|---|---|---|
| ● Freedom of choice | ● Freedom of choice as an absolute | ● Freedom of choice | ● Freedom as fulfilment |
| ● Equality of opportunity | ● Freedom before equality – inequality immutable fact of creation | ● Equality essentially utopian | ● Equality as egalitarianism |
| ● Meritocratic justice | ● Injustice only caused by wilful action | ● Justice defined as 'fairness' | ● Procedural justice for all |
| ● Tolerance and individual inter-relationship | ● Society unimportant | ● Fair treatment for all | ● Interdependence as co-operation |

# Biblical theology and the politics of the Centre

*Francis Bridger*

Theological perspectives on politics ● The theses and liberalism ● Liberalism: A theological evaluation ● Biblical freedom ● The individual and community ● Corporate motifs ● Left, Right, Centre? ● Conclusion.

In an age of widespread political cynicism and confusion, the thoughtful Christian finds it no less difficult to know how to vote than does a sizeable proportion of the electorate. By way of introduction, therefore, I should emphasize two points.

Firstly, in what follows I shall not seek to expound detailed policies of the Centre or any other party at the time of writing. Policies, understood as programmes for government, are notoriously shifting sands subject to contingencies which may change very quickly (as the Labour Party is currently discovering). I have consequently sought to make out a case in favour of the Centre over and against the Left and the Right on the basis of fundamental philosophy and beliefs; policy references, in so far as they occur at all, are used only to illustrate these.

The second point is that the reader will find throughout this essay the politics of the Centre referred to as liberalism. By this I do not simply mean the Liberal Party or the Liberal Democrats, but also the former SDP, all of whose philosophies may broadly be said to be liberal in their roots and fundamentals. Despite the socialist origins of the former SDP, and protestations to the contrary by some of its leaders, I would include it within this general ethos of liberalism. When I speak of liberalism, therefore, I am speaking of a phenomenon not a single party.

The starting point for political theology must be the Bible. But how does the Bible speak ethically? Although I agree with many of the opening theses which preface this book, I have serious reservations about one fundamental point. The theses appear to represent the view that biblical principles can be derived from particular verses of Scripture either individually or in aggregate. However attractive this view might seem, I believe it to be over simplistic and in danger of being misleading. I would contend that when we look closely, we find that the biblical writers arrive at conclusions about ethical matters far more by means of examples and perspectives than by abstract reasoning or appeals to free-standing principles. Put another way, the writers seem to say something like, 'Look, this is how God requires us to live. We can see what this means by considering how God acted in such and such a way at such and such a time in such and such a place.' In this manner they arrive at moral commands and obligations derived not from a system of principles but from a series of examples. In short, the obligation and historical example are interwoven in such a way that one is inseparable from the other.

I want to argue, therefore, that in taking the Bible seriously as God's word, we need to think of its ethical material in terms of examples and perspectives rather than principles. Having said this, however, I am aware that the propositional terms of the present debate have been set by the nature of the opening theses. While I would prefer to recast these along the lines of perspectives and examples, I have attempted in this essay to address the kind of questions set out in the theses as they stand.

I want to argue, therefore, not that the Bible should be downgraded (as some might fear from what I have just said) but that in taking it seriously as God's word, we need to think of its ethical material in terms of paradigms and perspectives rather than principles. My argument, in summary, is this: firstly, the notion of biblical principles as generally used should be treated with a great deal of caution. Secondly, a more biblical way of approaching ethics is to look for paradigms and examples in relevant areas. Thirdly, although this may give rise to general moral obligations, it is not always straightforward to translate these into specific political policies. Fourthly, a much more sophisticated hermeneutic is required to engage with biblical morality than can be supplied by the appeal to biblical principles.[1]

Having addressed, therefore, the prior question of how far theses 1–19 can be used politically, it now remains for us to turn to the question of how all this applies to contemporary British politics and particularly the politics of the Centre.

# Theological perspectives on politics

How and why the state should intervene in social and economic affairs is the central question of modern politics. It is, however, not a new question. The prophet Samuel warned the people of Israel that their clamour for a king would end in centralized tyranny such that 'When that day comes, you will cry out for relief from the king you have chosen' (1 Sa. 8:18). The problem of power, like the poor, has always been with us.

In theses 7–19 we have a series of answers to this question. Theses 7–12 advance a set of moral and theological propositions for political discussion. In so far as they express biblical perspectives, they speak with authority to issues of economic and social justice. But at first sight they appear simply to represent a pastiche of proof texts in support of views which bear remarkable resemblance to late twentieth-century bourgeois democracy. The critic might be forgiven for wondering whether the Bible is being used ideologically rather than critically.

If, however, they are understood as distillation statements of biblical paradigms, it becomes possible to view the theses somewhat differently: as attempts to produce action-guiding norms which lie mid-way between highly general values such as love and justice and very specific commands such as, 'When you reap the harvest of your land, do not reap to the very edges . . . Leave them for the poor and the alien' (Lv. 19:9–10).

Theses 13–19, on the other hand, put forward much more specific obligations. It is here that the culturally conditioned nature of the theses becomes most evident. In every thesis, for example, the dominating ethical category is that of rights – an acutely anachronistic category from a biblical perspective. The language of rights (at least in the modern sense) is decidedly not biblical and the philosophy which underlies it in modern discussion even less so. Yet theses 13–19 have borrowed so heavily from a post-Enlightenment world-view that they exemplify precisely the problem referred to earlier of absolutizing beliefs which are culturally relative.

Of course, it is possible that this may show nothing more than that the theses are culturally conditioned. But we need to recognize that to some extent this is bound to be true: all theological beliefs and statements are in some way the product of dialogue with contemporary culture and it would be strange if political theology did not share this characteristic.

The key question, then, is whether liberalism, or rather the version of it represented by the theses, is theologically justifiable. In answering this question, our task is threefold: firstly, to examine the theses to see if they really are a form of liberalism; secondly, to evaluate liberalism from a theological standpoint; and thirdly, to assess the philosophy and policies of the Centre against contemporary Conservatism and socialism.

# The theses and liberalism

The former leader of the Liberal Party, David Steel, has defined the philosophy of liberalism as:

> belief in the supreme value of the individual and the individual's freedom and rights; and a conviction that the only value of the state is to remove obstacles in the path of liberty and to create the positive conditions of freedom whereby human beings might realise their human potential to the full.[2]

He goes on to suggest that this definition entails a number of basic affirmations.

1. Government should be limited. The state is a necessary evil for the protection of the individual and the promotion of his or her well-being but it is the servant of individuals not the master.

2. The state should intervene in economic and social life to promote individual well-being but this should be kept to a minimum.

3. The purpose of the state should be to enhance and develop individual natural rights. These include the right to freedom of speech and association, the right to religious toleration, the right to trade and the rights of minorities.

4. Governments should be elected according to democratic means which reflect individual natural rights.

5. Governments must be subject to the rule of law.

6. Nations have the right to self-determination. This is analogous to the right of individuals to order their lives freely provided they do not undermine the freedoms of others.

When we compare these six characteristics with theses 1–19 we find a striking correspondence: theses 1 and 12 speak of the danger of arbitrary state power and the preference of the rule of law over the rule of personal whim. Thesis 2 speaks of the primacy of individual rights and goes on to list these in terms identical to 3 above. Thesis 7 defines freedom to trade as fundamental while thesis 12 asserts that to deny it is demonic. Thesis 2 speaks of the right of the individual to access to basic economic resources while theses 11 and 15 underline the responsibility of the state to intervene to safeguard this right and to protect those who have fallen into poverty. Theses 17–19 restate the classic liberal suspicion of centralized power by calling for a balance between centres of power such as government, businesses and trade unions in the interests of the individual consumer (a nice alliance here between historic liberal emphasis on individual freedom, and modern consumerism).

There are *prima facie* grounds, therefore, for claiming that Christian teaching as set out in the 19 theses can be closely correlated with the philosophy and goals of liberalism. Of course, the reasoning behind secular liberal philosophy and theses 1–19 is vastly different. The theses seek to ground their conclusions in theology while philosophical liberalism looks to non-theological assumptions about the nature of human beings as both individual and social creatures. Nevertheless, the political conclusions are much the same: protection of individual liberties, promotion of individual well-being within community and limited government.

# Liberalism: A theological evaluation

While space does not permit a thoroughgoing analysis of liberalism, any evaluation from a theological standpoint must examine at least the twin pillars on which liberalism rests: its conception of freedom, and its conception of the individual. From these follow its philosophy of society and social justice.

Freedom, like most large ideas, is a slippery term. It is invoked by Left, Right and Centre alike, and such is its emotive power that no politician can fail to identify himself or herself with it. In the pantheon of modern values, it occupies the topmost place. What, however, does it mean? And how can we evaluate the idea theologically?

The starting point for our thinking must be the contemporary context. All across the world freedom is hailed as the paramount goal of progressive societies. As I write, the Berlin Wall is being torn down and the post-war map of Europe redrawn in the name of democratic freedom. Nearer home, the rhetoric of the Thatcher era has been full of references to freedom: freedom from state control, freedom of the individual, and freedom from stifling bureaucracy, to mention but three.[3]

We need to be aware, however, that behind the bare notion of freedom lie two distinct and divergent concepts.[4] The first can be termed 'freedom from'. A benchmark definition of this idea has been provided by Friedrich Hayek and Sir Keith Joseph.[5] Both are renowned philosophers of the New Right and both have influenced Mrs Thatcher enormously, the latter serving in Thatcher Cabinets throughout the 1980s. The definition of freedom they offer is highly significant and goes a long way towards explaining the Conservative government's policies. In their view, freedom must be equated solely with *the absence of intentional coercion*. In other words, freedom is defined negatively: individuals may be regarded as free as long as no one is intentionally forcing them to do what they do not wish. This definition has far-reaching consequences.[6]

Firstly, it enables the New Right to distinguish between freedom and ability. The poor may be unable to afford decent housing (for example) but they are not in this way subject to coercion. No one is coercing them against their will by saying, 'You are not allowed to buy the home you want'.

Secondly, it follows that while the government must secure equal liberty in the sense of ensuring that coercion is removed, it has no duty to go any further in the name of freedom. On the Hayek-Joseph thesis, freedom is facilitated by passing laws which prevent people from being coerced. Laws which enforce redistribution of wealth, however, are themselves coercive since they take by force the resources of one group to give to another. By the same token, governmental aid to developing countries is contrary to liberty since it is likewise redistributionist. This restricted view of freedom has significant implications for social justice, as we shall see later.

The second concept of freedom may be characterized as 'freedom to'. This notion points to the self-evident fact that mere absence of coercion as understood by Joseph and Hayek is defective as a definition of true freedom. People can be just as trapped and coerced by poverty or by lack of dignity as by oppressive laws and institutions. The homeless family dependent on state benefits may be free from political tyranny but is in other no less real ways unfree, despite Sir Keith Joseph's contention that 'poverty is not unfreedom'. What such a family needs is the freedom to achieve self-worth, human dignity and participation in the ordinary life of the community. In other words, it needs *freedom from* poverty and dependence in order to find *freedom to* become fully responsible human beings. The two kinds of freedom are inextricably linked.

## Biblical freedom

From the standpoint of theological ethics, freedom is much more than the mere absence of coercion. In biblical terms, the paradigm of freedom is to be found in the story of the exodus.[7] Israel's liberation from slavery presents a model of freedom to which biblical writers in both Old and New Testaments return again and again. Thus the eighth-century prophets, facing a world of rapid economic change in which the institutions established in the Pentateuch were being swept away, issued a challenge in the name of Yahweh: the economic enslavement of whole strata of society by the newly enriched nobility must cease. Israelite families must be restored to the kind of economic and social independence envisaged in the pentateuchal legislation. It was God himself who originally gave them freedom from economic and political oppression by delivering them from Egypt. New slavery such as that practised by the *nouveau riche* entrepreneurial class (who had done rather well out of Israel's economic miracle) is a breach of the divine law.[8]

The implications of this theological conception of freedom were twofold. In the first place, the redemption of the nation from its slave status required that Israelites regard themselves as fundamentally equal before God and in relation to one another. The freedom which Yahweh had given had been achieved not by human endeavour but by divine grace. All were equal in sharing in this covenant freedom. 'Hence,' as Richard Bauckham has remarked, 'in Israel freedom entailed not inequality but equality.'[9]

Secondly, 'the law and the prophets were positively concerned with maintaining the economic independence of Israelite families, consisting in their inalienable right to share in the land which God had given to all Israel.'[10] The Old Testament makes it abundantly clear that the land was a sign of God's grace and it is in this context that the notion of rights must be understood.[11] It was not simply a parcel of resources to be carved up by the most able and talented or to be allocated according to the impersonal action of the market. It was a grace-gift given equally to all members of the covenant community, and in consequence all had a grace-right to share in it fairly.

The paradigm of social and political values we are given in Israel, therefore, points to much more than the market freedom espoused by the contemporary Conservative Party. The equal access to resources enshrined in the land legislation of the Pentateuch points not to the promotion of individualistic freedoms as envisaged by Hayek and Joseph (which easily become freedoms to exploit) but to a positive conception of liberty as freedom to engage in economic activity *as a member of the community*. This kind of freedom, however, entails community recognition that individuals and families must be given access to resources in order that they might play a part in the development of the community as a whole. In modern terms, they should not simply be left to fend for themselves on grudgingly-given reduced state benefits, but rather should be positively enabled to re-enter the economic life of the nation.

What this model does *not* point to, however, is a state-controlled economy. The Bible is too realistic about the corruptive effects of concentrations of power to lend support to a socialistic philosophy such as that practised until recently in communist countries, and to a lesser extent as advocated for much of the last decade by the Labour Party. What we seem to have in the Israel example is some kind of balance between the freedom of individuals and families to engage in economic life, and the responsibility of the community to enable them to do so. Although the modern notion of the state is foreign to biblical thinking, the implication for democratic societies is that the state, in its capacity as representative of the community, must act as the servant enabler.[12] This is precisely the role envisaged for the state by modern liberalism whether represented by the Liberal Democrats or the former SDP. It is not the kind of role envisaged by either Thatcherite Conservatism or the Labour Party for most of the 1980s. Whether, even now, the so-called 'modernized' Labour Party really believes in a decentralized, social market state is open to question. But I shall return to this point later.

In the New Testament we find the metaphor of freedom deepened and extended so that although used in a different way, it retains its force precisely because of its earlier political implications. Here it is freedom from sin and the powers and principalities which is given by God through Christ. Although it is not political freedom which Paul has in mind in Romans 6, political imagery is used to make a key point: that just as God gave liberty to the members of the covenant community of Israel, so he gives liberty in Christ to the members of the new covenant. The metaphor has not lost its power, but its context has changed.

In both the Old and New Testaments, this freedom was firmly rooted in the character and acts of God. It is highly significant that the Bible nowhere speaks of freedom as an abstraction, but always in terms of concrete, historical acts. Moreover, freedom from a biblical perspective is relational. It is a grace-gift given by God in relationship with his people and it serves to release them to live in love and service to him and to one another. It is not an abstract,

Platonic principle of the modern post-Enlightenment kind.

Before we pass to a consideration of liberalism's second great pillar, the value of the individual, we need to take the notion of positive freedom, or *freedom to*, one step further. If the role of the state is to enhance this kind of freedom, what is its theological basis? Richard Bauckham has suggested that in biblical terms, 'freedom from' (slavery in the Old Testament, sin in the New) always entails 'freedom to'. But freedom to what purpose? The answer is freedom to serve others and to love God. The love of neighbour enjoined by the levitical code and reaffirmed by Jesus is in fact a freedom for the sake of others. Freedom is a positive caring for others. He writes, 'My neighbour is not simply a restraint on my freedom but one whom I am to love as myself' (Lv. 19:18). The New Testament's understanding of freedom as not so much *from* others as *for* others is already implicit in the Old Testament sense of social responsibility.[13]

It is precisely this equation of freedom with service that is light years away from current Conservative philosophy. It does, however, lie at the heart of modern liberalism. And it is the belief that the state must intervene (albeit minimally) to ensure this positive freedom that makes liberalism coherent with a biblical perspective, and which at the same time distinguishes it from Thatcherism.

## The individual and community

Discussion of freedom inevitably leads to a consideration both of the individual and of community. Here we must note two strands in the development of liberalism. The first is represented by the nineteenth-century philosopher John Stuart Mill, who argued that morally and politically the individual must be regarded as paramount.[14] Society is artificial in that it is formed by the free association of individuals who consent to put themselves under collective government for their own individual sakes. Society is not natural by virtue of being part of the natural order (in contrast to families). It is created by individual human wills, and consequently must be subject to them. The purpose of government is to free the individual from unnecessary constraints, and to promote conditions which will enable the rational individual to make his or her own choices. Government is essentially a referee between competing individuals. On this version, society is nothing more than a collection of atomistic, autonomous individuals whose interests must take priority over any conception of the general, collective good.

This form of liberalism, as we have seen, finds expression within the present Conservative Party much more than within the parties of the Centre. This is because both the Liberal Democrats and the former SDP have adopted a contrary strand of philosophical liberalism known as *communitarian liberalism*.

Communitarian liberalism, as its name implies, rejects the atomistic assumptions of the school represented by John Stuart Mill. Instead it argues that individuals must be understood as persons-in-relation. The individual self is a 'located' self. Individuals do not exist as abstract entities but as persons whose individual identities have been formed by being in relation with others. As Michael Sandel puts it:

> I am situated from the start, embedded in a history which locates me among others, and implicates my good in the good of the communities whose stories I share.[15]

Freedom and community are thus inextricably linked within communitarian liberalism. The individual is not free to pursue his or her own interests at the expense of others. There is a corporate identity which belongs to a nation, society or community which is more than the sum of individual identities. Such an identity arises out of the complex network of beliefs, values, social meanings and relationships which go to make up the sense of oneness we call community. The notion of society as no more than a collection of self-determining individuals is thus a fallacy.

The communitarian conception stands in stark contrast to modern Conservatism with its emphasis upon the priority of individuals over and against society (even to the point of Mrs Thatcher's claim that there is no such thing as society). Because of this contrast we can see clearly how great is the gulf between the parties of the Centre and the Tory Party of the New Right. As David Owen has argued:

> What is needed is a political philosophy outside the restricted confines of much of the present polarised political debate ... which revives the concept of fellowship and community within a participatory democratic society and which sees change not as a threat but as a challenge.[16]

But how far is communitarian liberalism theologically warrantable? After all, Mrs Thatcher herself has made considerable claims for individualism in the name of the Bible and Christian theology.

## Corporate motifs

Within Scripture, the relationship between the individual and the community is defined by a number of what we might call 'corporate motifs'.[17] We can only touch upon these in the barest detail but even this will enable us to see that both the radical individualism of the New Right and the traditional collectivism of the Left are theologically deficient.

### a. The image of God
The statement in Genesis 1:26–27 that God made human beings in his own image is at one and the same time exhilarating and enigmatic. Theologians have long been divided as to what the image actually consists in but at the present time three suggestions lead the field.[18] Firstly, the image has been taken to refer to certain God-given characteristics such as moral capacity or rationality which set

human beings apart from the rest of creation. This interpretation was widely held among medieval scholastics and a number of modern Reformed theologians.

Secondly, it has been argued that the image refers to human dominion over creation. This view is based upon the fact that in the Genesis account, the creation of humanity takes place as the summit of God's activity. He expressly gives Adam and Eve responsibility over the created order. It is also a fact that archaeological evidence from the Middle East confirms that it was a common practice for kings to demonstrate their rule by erecting statues bearing their image. In this way, their subjects were constantly reminded of the king's dominion over them.

The third interpretation, identified with Martin Luther, locates the divine image in God's relationship to his creatures. Adam and Eve possessed the divine image by virtue of their relationship to God. The fall marred but did not utterly destroy this relationship, and hence the image is seen as continuing in Genesis 9:6.

Whichever one of these interpretations is adopted, it seems clear that the image of God is corporate. Significantly, in Genesis 1:26, God says 'Let us make man in our image', which some commentators have taken as a reference to the three persons of the Trinity. But even if this is not a Trinitarian reference, it is further significant that the image is given to man and woman together as representatives of the whole of humanity. It is this which has reinforced in Christian social theology the belief in universal human dignity.

When we turn to the New Testament we find Paul speaking in similar terms of the image of Christ. Sinful humanity is redeemed through and in Christ so as to bring into being a new humanity. But we need to note that this is not a humanity divided solely into individual units: it is a new community of persons-in-relationship. The corporate language of Genesis is reworked along Christological lines to give a picture of humanity as inherently corporate as well as individual.

## b. The covenant people

We have already noted the importance of solidarity as a social and moral concept in the Old Testament. We have seen, also, how this sprang from God's redemption of Israel from Egypt and the subsequent establishment of the nation with laws embodying this decisive act of grace. What is no less important is that in Old Testament terms the nation was bound together not only by its shared experience and memory of salvation but by its covenant with God.[19] Individuals and families are understood to hold responsibility for one another by virtue of belonging to the same covenant people: the people which God himself chose and blessed, not as isolated individuals, but as his extended family.

This solidarity imposed considerable obligations upon the people of Israel. They were not allowed to sell one another into slavery, to deprive one another of their God-given land rights, or to lend money at interest.[20] Positively, the nation as a whole had a duty to care for the poor, the dispossessed and the powerless as typified by the orphans and widows. One would no more think of charging interest on a loan to a stranger or allowing a stranger to starve than allowing the same to happen to a member of one's own family. In every important social sense the stranger *was* a member of the covenant family.

Again this strong notion of corporate identity and solidarity is alien to the modern industrialized world, and particularly to the philosophy of Thatcherism. We cannot go into the complex social and historical reasons for this, but if we are to take seriously the values expressed in the covenant concept, we are forced to question whether the philosophy of individualism espoused by the New Right can reasonably be held to represent biblical perspectives.

Biblical thinking, however, is also alien to socialist collectivism, with its emphasis upon the subordination of the individual to the state and the growth of centralized state power. The biblical paradigms embody respect for personal liberty while at the same time affirming the obligation of the individual to the life of the community. The relationship is not one-sided, either in favour of the individual (as in modern Conservatism) or in favour of the state (as in socialism). It is reciprocal (as in communitarian liberalism).

*c. The body of Christ*

Although the body analogy of 1 Corinthians 12 – 14 is first and foremost addressed to the church, at the same time it looks outwards to the world. It does so by serving as a model for social relationships: the church is portrayed as the bridgehead of the age to come. In the same way that Old Testament Israel embodied the values of the kingdom of God, so the church does the same. Paul's teaching on the body is therefore relevant to political as well as to church life.

John Atherton has identified interdependence as the key aspect of Paul's use of the body metaphor.[21] The members of the body are separate but united. They exist in unity by virtue of the unity which is found in Christ and which is celebrated in the Eucharist. The bread and wine remain visible signs of our oneness in Christ so that we can never forget that by God's grace we are one body serving one Lord.

This does not preclude the exercise of individual gifts and creativity. Members of the body have complementary gifts and callings which should not conflict but which should work together for the mutual upbuilding of the whole. Thus Paul strikes a balance between individuality and corporateness. Complementarity, moreover, involves the integration of unequals into a single unified whole. Different members of the body may possess different gifts and feel unequal in status but, as Paul makes clear, each contributes to the life of the body. 'All are primarily full members of the Body irrespective of the apparent or real significance of their contribution.'[22]

This leads to a third feature of complementarity: solidarity in the face of vulnerability. If a member of the body is under threat, the whole body is affected. Individual members cannot act as if others did not matter. Each is responsible for the others: 'If one part suffers, every part suffers with it' (1 Cor. 12:26).

What are the political implications of all this? It should

not be thought that Paul is talking here only about the internal relationships of the church. In Pauline theology, the church is the first-fruits of the kingdom of Christ. The life of the body of Christ is therefore a sign to the world that God's rule has arrived and is in action. This eschatological dimension of Paul's ecclesiology means that the church can never regard itself as a sect. It cannot isolate itself from the world since it is meant to be a sign of the new world.[23] Moreover, its values and practices are intended to demonstrate the goal of God's redemption: a recreated humanity in Christ.

Paul's teaching thus provides us with a number of paradigms by which to evaluate political philosophies and policies. If these contradict the goals and values revealed in Christ's purpose for his body, then they must be seriously questioned. If, however, they move towards the goal of a society which embodies the values of the kingdom then they are to be welcomed. Taking into account the nature of the body metaphor and the sense of corporate solidarity to which it points, it seems clear that Christians must be committed to a society in which the ethos of mutual care takes precedence over possessive individualism, in which the state as the protector of the weak must act to secure their basic needs and access to resources, and in which such action is seen as a welcome responsibility, not a grudging duty. On these criteria, it is hard to see how contemporary Conservatism can be regarded as truly biblical, whatever the personal piety of individual Conservatives.

### d. The kingdom of God

Like the body, the kingdom is a motif for solidarity. It is also a motif for justice and righteousness. A number of recent studies have shown that the kingdom is a concept which can neither be restricted to individual interior faith nor to a state of affairs which will come solely in the future.[24] It has already burst into the life of the world. This means that the paradigm of the kingdom offered first by Israel and then by the New Testament churches must be taken seriously in contemporary politics.

112

To say this is not to retreat into some kind of millenarian fantasy. History is littered with examples of those.[25] Nor is it to suppose that the kingdom will be built by human endeavour independent of the gracious activity of God. Nor will it be achieved this side of the parousia. Rather it is a matter of seeking to order societies (*i.e.* conduct politics) in such a way that the values of the kingdom will be enacted as far as possible within a sinful world which awaits its redemption.

Foremost of these values is justice. The ruler, according to both the Old and New Testaments, is obligated to act justly to ensure the protection of the vulnerable. In this way the justice of God will be upheld.[26]

In recent years it has become increasingly difficult to see how this concept of justice can be reconciled with government policies. The policies of the Thatcher decade have produced not only unprecedented prosperity but also unprecedented inequalities coupled with record levels of poverty. Whole strata of society have been excluded from the economic processes which enable people to contribute to the common good. This has been accompanied by an official attitude towards the poor which has either denied that poverty really exists, or has deliberately reduced welfare benefits in order to cut government spending. All this has been cloaked in high sounding moral language such as 'reducing people's dependency on the state', or 'enabling people to stand on their own feet'. The truth of the matter has been that the poor have suffered the double indignity of paying the price for the so-called economic miracle of the 1980s and of being treated as outcasts. Far from seeing itself as the willing protector of the poor, the Conservative government has begrudged its role in supplying even minimal support. The question must be asked how this is supposed to fit with the values of the kingdom.

### e. *The incarnation and Trinity*
The doctrines of the incarnation and the Trinity provide us with further clues as to God's purpose for human society. Together they supply a radical critique both of individualism and of collectivism.

The incarnation makes it clear that God loves the whole of his creation. By taking flesh he reaffirmed the Genesis declaration that God saw everything and it was good. Moreover, by sending his Son in the form of sinful human beings, he identified with the material nature of humanity and the world in which we live. In doing so, he showed once and for all that to be 'in Christ' is to be committed to the wholeness of the created order.

Once we realize this, we see that just as God gave himself on behalf of his creation, so we are likewise called to love what (and whom) he has made and redeemed. As Kenneth Leech has commented:

> A major consequence of taking incarnational faith seriously is that the spiritual person, far from despising , or fearing or withdrawing from the world, needs to be inflamed by a passionate and intense love for the world, seeing in the material things of the world the handiwork of God, and in the people of the world the face of Christn.[27]

The Christian, then, is committed to politics by virtue of his or her commitment to the incarnate Christ. For it is only through political action that the world of human activity, relationships and life can be loved for its own sake and people loved as God loves them. Put simply, if God loves humanity so must we.

But what political form should this love take? It is here that the doctrine of the Trinity points to a communitarian model which rules out New Right individualism *tout court*. The basis for this contention is that the Trinity in itself comprises a community of persons which in turn provides us with a paradigm of social life. Leonardo Boff identifies the characteristics of the Trinitarian relationship as dialogue, communion, reciprocity, self-giving and mutual love. The persons of the Godhead do not exist as independent persons living for themselves but rather

the essential characteristic of each Person is to

> be *for* the others, *through* the others, *with* the
> others and *in* the others. They do not exist in
> themselves, for themselves: the 'in themselves'
> is 'for the others'.[28]

When we apply this to human social relationships, we are
faced with a very different picture from that drawn by
New Right individualists. The communion of the divine
persons points to the truth that 'individuals need to
remain always within a network of relationships and
society needs to be a conjuncture of relationships of communion and participation'.[29] Thus, 'the Trinity can be
seen as the model for any just, egalitarian (while respecting differences) social organisation'.[30] 'Communion is
the first and last word about the mystery of the Trinity.
Translating this truth of faith into social terms, we can say
"the Trinity is our true social programme".'[31]

But if this rules out individualism, it also rules out
collectivism which disregards the uniqueness and dif-
ferentiation of persons. Socialist regimes fail to recognize
that communion of persons within political society
requires

> going through the essential process of accep-
> ting differences between persons and com-
> munities ... Bureaucratic imposition of the
> social dimension does not produce a society of
> equality within the bounds of respect for differ-
> ences, but one of collectivization with elements
> of massification.[32]

This would seem to leave only one model which fits
with a Trinitarian perspective: that of the communitarian
liberal.

If anything seems clear from our discussion so far, it is
that the balance between individual liberty (understood
as freedom *for* others), and corporate responsibility for
individual well-being, lies at the heart of theological
motifs of community and biblical notions of justice. Theology which is biblical endorses neither an individualistic

free-for-all nor a regime of state control. Rather, it is concerned that, while individuals should develop a sense of personal responsibility for others, and while the state should foster this through political and economic intervention where necessary, the realities of power require that the power of the state should be limited. It is hard, on this basis, to see how the philosophy and policies of the Thatcher administrations or the collectivism of the 1980s Labour Party can be reckoned to fit best with this perspective.

# Left, Right, Centre?

Where does this leave us? It will be clear by now that, in my view, the most complimentary thing that can be said about New Right Conservatism is that it is seriously defective. Its conception of freedom and the relationship of the individual to the community are fundamentally unbiblical and unwarrantable. Moreover, when we take into account the paradigm offered by the social model of the Trinity we can see the deep deficiency of New Right individualism.

When we turn to communitarian liberalism, however, we should not be naive about its philosophical or technological basis. I am not seeking to argue that it is really a disguised form of Christian theology. Nonetheless, I would argue that there is a greater congruence between its model of social life and the model provided by Christian theology than that of contemporary Conservatism or socialism. The upbuilding of the individual in community, the strengthening of individual and social relationships, the acceptance of differences between individuals, the recognition of the principle of complementarity, the enabling of people to develop complementary gifts and abilities, are all fundamentally liberal values. In so far as these values have historically found a place within Conservatism or socialism they have done so having flowed from the fountainhead of liberalism. Likewise, the liberalism I represent requires as a precondition the recognition of universal human worth and dignity, and the creation of economic and social conditions which enhance that dignity. Put another way, the Christian belief in social justice and righteousness is mirrored in the concern of communitarian liberalism to work for just and participatory societies.

But what about the Labour Party? As I have argued above, there has been a tendency within socialist ideology and policies to mirror the individualistic imbalance of the Right with a collectivist imbalance of the Left. Moreover, the history of the Labour governments of the 1960s and 1970s has been to promote increasing concentrations of power in non-elected, extra-Parliamentary bodies such as trade unions and the bureaucracy. It is only a few years since we were faced with a Labour government paralysed by this process.

It is still too early to tell whether the policy review *Meet the Challenge, Make the Change* published by the Labour Party in 1989 does anything more than disguise the underlying collectivist nature of the party. I, for one, am suspicious. There are at least two plausible readings of Labour revisionism and it is not always clear which is the more likely.

The first reading runs something like this. Labour, under the impact of three election defeats, has returned to its true place on the Centre-Left of British politics. The period from 1980 to 1987 must be viewed as an aberration. The party was temporarily deranged by Tony Benn and co. The trauma of the SDP split in 1981 created conditions under which the Left could triumph, but now the Left are in decline as Labour tacks back towards its authentic historical position and the SDP has collapsed. The role of the policy review, on this interpretation, is twofold: to construct moderate policies which take account of the changed national and international conditions; and to signal to the world that Labour has turned its back on the Left.

But what about the second reading? This is far more sceptical. 'Is it really credible,' say suspicious people like me, 'that the Labour leadership, all of whom fought the last general election on policies diametrically opposed to those now being espoused, have turned their backs on all they once held dear? And what about those who fought the 1983 election on a manifesto which proclaimed the virtues of nationalization, high taxation, unilateral nuclear disarmament, opposition to the Common Market and so on?' It was Denis Healey who later described this as the longest suicide note in history but it was Neil Kinnock who once proclaimed its virtues.

So my critical faculties make me wonder which is the real Labour Party and which is the authentic socialism: the party and the policies of 1983 and 1987 or the party and policies of 1989? Moreover, have those hard left MPs elected in 1987 and all those leftist constituency parties of which we heard so much evaporated overnight? My observation at the local level is that they are simply lying low in the drive for electoral success. In short, I believe in conversion but I am not sure the Labour Party's present stance is more than electorally convenient window dressing and I suspect there are many true socialist believers (some of them in positions of leadership at national and local level) who are simply biding their time.

# Conclusion

I have tried to show how biblical examples and perspectives supply a critique of both the Left and the Right in British politics. I am not naive about the parties of the Centre (who could be after the experience of 1987–88?) but for the reasons I have cited above, I would argue that the theological perspectives expressed in the 19 theses are best represented by the historic tradition of communitarian liberalism than by either contemporary Conservatism or contemporary socialism.

# A Conservative view of the policy of full employment: a case study

## Sir Fred Catherwood

Incomes policies ● Monetary policies ● Industry on a human scale ● Christian principles ●
The desire for power ● The advantage of small
companies ● Small and medium-sized enterprises ● The diffusion of economic power

I find no problem in agreeing all the objectives set out in
the first set of propositions and little difficulty with the
second and third set of objectives. My wording might be
different, but not on political grounds.

To those of us engaged in the cut and thrust of politics,
the problems come when agreed objectives clash with
each other, or when the general good runs into legitimate
vested interests, or into the darker side of human nature,
to which even Moses, that greatest of lawgivers, had to
make some concessions.

Rather than range over the whole of economic policy, it
may be helpful to look at the conflict between one policy
with which all Christians should agree, and other very
desirable policies. If we believe that we are made in the

image of God the creator, that we are all stewards of God's world, that each of us has a talent which it is our duty to use to the full, then we must agree that Christians, above all people, should be committed to a policy of full employment. Other economic aims may be desirable, but the right and duty of each man and woman to use and develop their talents must be central.

Let's look at the way in which other policies may conflict with this central policy.

There is a consensus in most countries still influenced by Christian ethics that the state should be responsible for social security. Usually the cost is added to the wages which employers have to pay. Other countries add it to taxes of one kind or another. In one way or another this puts up the cost to the employer of giving employment, so there is some level of cost which puts at risk the other social objective of full employment.

In similar countries there are also policies for fair wages. It is agreed, for example, that employers should pay a minimum level of wage. But this can cut the number of jobs which employers can offer and also increases unemployment. There is also, following the Christian principle that wages should be 'fair and equal', a practice of giving the same 'rate for the job' regardless of age. But this means that employers are inclined to prefer experienced people over inexperienced for the same rate, which, in times of unemployment, makes it much harder for the young to find work.

Full employment must also be balanced against the right to free collective bargaining. Those societies most strongly influenced by Christian values believe that it is not enough to say that relations between employer and employee must be free and contractual. The bargaining power of individual employees must also be strengthened so that they can bargain on equal terms with employers and have the right, as an ultimate sanction, to withdraw their labour. These rights legitimized the trade unions. Great Britain has made laws to regulate their powers and to see that the leaders are responsible to their members.

Those unions with greater bargaining power, however,

will tend to get higher wages at the expense of those with less. Britain has also found more recently that the objective of a trade union to use the bargaining power of its stronger members to help to get the same 'rate for the job' for its weaker members has been corrupted by small groups of workers with especially strong bargaining power who, by unofficial strikes, get more money for themselves without the help of the union. This process has created serious wage-led inflation, which diverts to consumption the funds which are needed to maintain employment, producing a malign combination of rising inflation and rising unemployment.

In most countries influenced by Christian ethics this pattern now undermines government's prime economic policy of full employment. In the last two decades, the central economic aim of such governments has been to find a way of restoring full employment.

There have been three different ways in which governments in different countries have tried to bring inflation under control and to restore full employment.

## Incomes policies

The first attempt, started in the 1960s, was through incomes policies. Governments laid down norms for wage increases which were negotiated with the trade unions at national level. Trade unions, believing that, as inflation was kept under control, government would use demand management to expand the economy, restore employment and increase output, undertook to negotiate within these norms.

This policy assumed, however, that the problem lay in the wage increases negotiated at national level and not in the pressure of unofficial settlements at plant level. But by the late 1960s it had become clear that nationally negotiated norms were being broken at plant level and, in Britain, the new Conservative government abandoned incomes policies when it came to power in 1970. It restored them two years later, but in 1974 it resigned and fought an election on an attempt by the miners to break the national norms. It lost the election, the incoming Labour government settled with the miners and the other unions followed the mining settlement. This eventually produced a currency crisis. The Labour government imposed its own incomes policy after being forced to borrow from the International Monetary Fund to save the currency. But, in the 'winter of discontent' in 1978–79, that policy was broken and the 1979 Conservative government set its face against incomes policies. Does that rule out incomes policies, or should we learn from the lessons of the past and build a better policy?

There is a strong moral case for an incomes policy. For Christians who believe the apostle Paul's command that wages should be 'just and equal' there must be a moral case for the two corresponding trade union bargaining principles, 'the rate for the job' and 'parity'. It can be argued that, with the lessons we have learnt, we should be able to create a national policy under which most wage-earners would feel their wage differentials took into account all their training, responsibilities, efforts and risks.

No doubt, too, the first three incomes policies were crude crisis efforts to keep down wages. In the process, it is clear that this squeeze on traditional differentials was what, in the end, destroyed them. The bargaining process in most major industries has mutually agreed and long-established differentials between all the different classes of job. These differentials have remained in place over long periods and through considerable changes in the national economy. What is missing in the massive creaking process of the annual wage round is machinery to deal with cases where the differential between one great bargaining circle and another has got out of line, where the Civil Service, teachers, coal miners or engineers believe that they now have a strong case for a higher *relative* increase.

The miners striking in 1973, for instance, knew that their differential had slipped badly during the run-down of the coal industry in the previous ten years. They believed that, with the steep rise in the cost of oil, the country was now more dependent on coal, and that their traditional differential should be restored. The incomes policy in force was more concerned with national norms than with differentials and the government believed that an increase for the miners would blow a hole in the incomes policy through which all other industries would crowd. So the Trades Union Congress made an offer to recognize that any increase awarded to the miners above the national norm would be acknowledged by the other unions as a restoration of the miners' differential and not as a basis of claims in the next wage round. In the event the government decided to hold an election and the offer was not put to the test.

The question is whether machinery, which dealt fairly with differentials and had more goodwill on both sides, would have established a sound long-term incomes policy, which could have dealt with major structural changes on differentials.

The Labour government had made considerable concessions to the trade unions in return for their acceptance of their second incomes policy. Direct taxation was raised to heights unknown in peacetime. Controls were put on prices which seemed more effective than the controls on wages, squeezing the cashflow which companies needed to invest and expand. But the explosion which ended the policy was caused by the renewed squeeze on the differentials of skilled workers. So the Conservative government in 1979 was reinforced in the belief that an incomes policy was simply not manageable, nor did it appear in the election manifestos of the Labour Party in 1983 or 1987.

The British had gone further than most other countries in formal incomes policies, but smaller countries, such as Sweden and the Netherlands, had less formal arrangements. The Federal Republic of Germany used its much more organized trade union system – with one union to an industry, and union participation in the upper tier company board – to get agreement on the rate of wage increase which the country could afford without inflation. But in the 1980s there was a swing in all of Western Europe against incomes policies, because it was clear that there was an underlying pressure of inflation which they did not touch. In one country after another there was a political swing to monetary policies of one kind or another. In Britain only the centre parties remained as advocates of incomes policies.

# Monetary policies

The crudest advocates of monetary policies argued that if government limited the increase in the supply of money to the level of expansion which the economy could afford, then companies would not be able to find the money to pay excessive wages and, with a slight time-lag, the growth of the economy would come into line with the funds available to finance it. Not many governments believed that it was quite so easy or that this mechanism would be fail-safe, but there was a strong feeling that the market sector, on which countries depended to pay their way in the world, had been squeezed by steady increases in the public sector. It was also believed that a similar ratchet effect worked on wage bargaining – big increases in good times, and no adjusting standstill in bad – was the primary cause of the increase in unemployment, which in Britain had risen from a quarter of a million in the 1950s to one and a half million by the end of the 1970s.

Whatever the merits or demerits of monetary policy, it was put to the test in Britain at the very moment when the second oil price increase sent a great shock wave through the international economy. Britain was especially hard hit. North Sea oil, which was just coming on stream, sent the pound up by 20% at the same time as the wage bill had gone up by 25%. So costs in British companies rose by 45%, far more than the costs of their international competitors. The consequent 20% drop in Britain's share of world trade, combined with the international recession, doubled the number out of work to three million.

No doubt there will come a time when the monetarists

will say that, in these circumstances, their policy never had a chance. It is noticeable, however, that, even with three million unemployed, and the lowest pressure on the economy for forty years, wages continued to rise at twice the rate of inflation. More remarkable, these wage increases were paid by companies under the greatest squeeze on their margins for forty years. Companies which were clearly headed for bankruptcy were paying amounts which could only bring the end nearer. Unions in companies which were headed for massive redundancy were making claims which could only bring nearer the loss of their members' jobs.

It is clear that after a decade of monetarism, and with eight years for the effects of the second oil shock to wear off, the disciplines of monetarism cannot restore employment either in Britain or in the rest of Europe – and it can be argued that America, with its huge deficit financing, never tried it. Monetarism may have negative advantages as a discipline to moderate inflation, but Christians must look for policies which will get our unemployed back to work.

# Industry on a human scale

Since the 1980s governments have begun to believe that small business rather than big business is the source of future jobs. Even big business itself is expanding through small operations. There is a compelling logic behind this.

Once the average business or plant grows to over 200 employees, time lost in strikes begins to rise. At 500 employees the line of the graph for time lost in strikes begins to climb, at 1000 employees it is climbing steeply, and at 5000 employees it is climbing almost vertically.

Bargaining becomes impersonal and formal in companies or plants of over 500 employees, especially where there is autonomous plant bargaining. The relationship is contractual, and there is no obligation on the employee to stay if he or she can get better pay somewhere else. So the bargain is for the maximum which the employer can be persuaded to pay, without too much regard for the consequences to the particular company for which the employee is working. Once a wage rate or an agreement on hours or conditions has been gained, it is entrenched. There is flexibility upwards but never downwards. To create the flexibility needed to stay in business, management stops recruiting and substitutes machines for people.

Of course the good trade union, negotiating for its members throughout industry, will try to take into account the effect of a wage award on the ability of the industry to compete. But in the late 1960s, it became apparent that the unions were losing control. The 'going rate' in the wage round was being settled on the shop-floor of some of the big plants, where unofficial pressure was bringing increases which no union boss would have considered possible. The effect on all industrial economies was the same. The phenomenon became known as 'cost push inflation' or, more commonly, as 'shop-floor power'.

Economists found it hard to analyse this phenomenon. Companies which were vulnerable to this pressure did not want to advertise it, nor did they want to explain to any outsider why they were vulnerable, because the figures were frightening. Shop-floor power affected some industries more than others.

A daily newspaper is a perishable commodity. There is nothing less saleable than yesterday's paper. If 10,000 papers missed a train, they were lost. At the point at which the presses started to run, most of the money had been spent. The few minutes on the presses were all that stood between the paper and the money to pay for the costs. At this point a walk-out by the men on the presses faced the management with a loss of revenue about sixty times the cost of the claim which they faced. Most papers paid up and, since there was no international competition, production wages on daily papers were several times the national average. But competition from TV closed several papers. Finally managements dismissed entire workforces and brought in new technology which automated most of the production work.

Big food manufacturers, with national advertising and a market share to protect, calculate that the cost of recovering market share after a strike would be maybe forty times the cost of the wage award for which they can settle. So the production line of the nationally marketed product is also very vulnerable to a stoppage.

A major car manufacturer makes huge investments in new technology, new design, new production lines and national advertising. Only the cost of the direct workers on the production line remains, and only they stand between the corporation and the income which is needed to cover the 90% of the costs which have already been incurred. A car is not as perishable as a newspaper and the balance of disadvantage depends on whether there are thousands of unsold cars in stock. If there are, then the company can afford a walk-out, but if it can sell every car produced, then it cannot. It has sometimes seemed that the 'going rate' for the wage round was settled by the number of cars in stock for the first car assembly plant to settle the wage package after the summer break.

If those with strong bargaining power get most, and those who cannot hold a production line to ransom get less, then, in wage settlements, might is right. The teacher, whose strike only sends the children home to the parents, and the nurse, who will not leave her patients, have no bargaining power, nor has the soldier or the policeman. Farm workers, shop and office workers (except those in the computer room) and restaurant workers cannot impose costs of thousands of pounds a minute by a walk-out. Those in declining industries do not do so well as those in booming industries. Those who have studied at university and done a long professional apprenticeship at low wages are often poorer than production workers in a big plant.

One answer, both Christian and practical, lies in organizing production on a human scale in units which work as a team, where management and other workers can know and learn to trust each other.

## Christian principles

If we go back to the Old Testament economy, we find an idealized picture of every man under his own vine and under his own fig-tree, owning his family's own inalienable means of production. Isaiah warned a generation hundreds of years later who were ignoring the laws which protected each family's means of independent production, 'Woe to you who join . . . field to field till no space is left and you live alone in the land. The LORD Almighty has declared in my hearing: ". . . A ten-acre vineyard will produce only a bath of wine, a homer of seed only an ephah of grain"' (Is. 5:8,9).[1]

Of course that was an agrarian economy, with famine and high infant mortality. To cure the sick and feed the hungry with the aid of science, we may need to work in bigger teams. But the principle of controlling our own means of livelihood is a good one and we should take note of the legal rights which safeguarded it and enabled an Israelite to avoid becoming a dependent servant. Naboth died rather than sell his family patrimony to King Ahab – who should never have asked for it (1 Ki. 21).

There are other useful Old Testament principles too. Samuel warned Israel against the concentration of power in a king, who would enslave them in order to enrich himself and to establish his military power (1 Sa. 8). Wise though Solomon was, he built up a huge impersonal administrative structure and, on his death, eight of the ten tribes repudiated his political system and seceded.

The apostles set up a church in which power was diffused and the New Testament letters are more by way of appeals than orders. But after Constantine recognized the Christian faith, the secular concentration of power in the emperor was reflected in the papal power over the church.

After the reformation of the church in the sixteenth century, and the diffusion of church power in the seventeenth, the countries of the Reformation moved slowly and surely towards the diffusion of political power, first to the middle classes and then to universal suffrage. The United States embodies this diffusion of power in the constitution.

## The desire for power

The power which corrupted the Jewish kings, the Roman emperors and the Papacy still corrupts. The bigger an organization and the more distant it is from the people it is supposed to serve, the more it becomes an end in itself. The reason why companies and plants get bigger and bigger has very often little to do with economics. It has much more to do with the desire for power, prestige and security. In the battles for power, the individual suffers.

When we read in the press of take-over battles, of whole organizations of thousands of workers being bought and sold as if they were no more than commodities; of great financial institutions selling their control to the highest bidder without a thought for the people who have given a working life to them, can we believe that that is right? More recently, when the tycoons cheat each other and cheat their shareholders, their aim is a power base from which to enrich themselves even further. It is not to improve economic performance.

Business should be controlled by those who understand the trade and not by people who have bought it for a financial speculation and are not committed to it any longer than the day when the share price shows them a profit. But even more important, the buying and selling of companies undermines the credibility of the professional managers who run them. Negotiations between management and workers need a high degree of trust. How can workers believe that the management will honour their undertakings if they are liable to be replaced by another management team as soon as the financial institutions sell out? A keen executive chairman once asked, 'Why don't the unions trust me?' The answer was that the life expectancy of an executive chairman in that company was three years.

## The advantage of small companies

Whatever the moral questions, however, can small companies survive in a world of international giants?

Although big corporations can be powerful, they are also vulnerable. The balance of competitive advantage is not always to the big company. A small company which is near to the customer, without any of the self-perpetuating overhead organization of the big company, can run rings round its giant rivals. Small companies do not need to dominate a market to expand their business. Their prices can be much more flexible, and they can pick up new business wherever the giant corporation is most inflexible.

In the last few years, about 400 small companies have started around the University of Cambridge. They are nearly all in high-technology such as computers, electronics, medical equipment, bio-technology and communications. They do not need the research laboratories of the huge companies; they are at the leading edge of technology themselves. They do not need the export organizations of the giants either. They deal directly with their agents in European and North American cities. No one ever reads of a strike in one of these companies. While big companies are declaring redundancies, they are taking on new workers. Nor do these companies need special government finance to get them going. They usually start by finding a new product which will meet a known gap in the market and then finding the first customers. After that the finance is no problem and the company is in business.

There is no reason why the friendly and helpful relationship between the University of Cambridge and these high-tech companies should not be repeated around other universities. Why shouldn't the great fund of potential innovation in university research be tapped by whole new generations of academic entrepreneurs? There is no reason why thousands of small high-tech companies should not be the leading edge of the country's economic growth as well as of its innovation.

Even in more mundane industries, advances in technology have made the big plant obsolete. A company's daily orders can be allocated by computer to give optimum daily production runs in scattered plants. Quality control can be built into the machine in a small plant and does not require the supervisory structure of a large plant. Present communications systems have returned us to small scale production.

Mass production may be seen, in retrospect, to be no more than an uncomfortable stage in the process of industrialization. No one regrets the passing of the 'dark satanic mill'. Similarly no one will regret the passing of the huge impersonal plant which, at a stage of development, produced at a cost which brought a wide range of products within reach of everyone. But as incomes increase, society wants more variety, for instance in the food it eats. Specialized products and specialized shops to sell them are far more common and small specialized companies are meeting the growing demand.

## Small and medium-sized enterprises

Government policies all over Europe now recognize 'Small and medium-sized enterprises' – or SMEs as they are called for short. Tax policies are now aimed to favour the SME and some of the huge pension advantage given to those who work in big corporations has been taken away. No longer is there the same strong tax incentive to stay bound to the same big company for a lifetime. The reduction of direct taxation helps those who want to set up their own business; the reduction of capital transfer tax helps to keep the family business going and avoids the strong temptation of family businesses to sell out as the only way of cashing in on the success of the business. New tax schemes help to find the outside risk money which small businesses need as they expand.

The view that the SME rather than the big corporation is critical to the future creation of jobs is based on rough evidence, not yet on systematic economic analysis. Once the evidence firms up, the next stage will be to see what can be done to limit the conglomeration of economic power in fewer and fewer hands. Already there is a feeling that the privatization of nationalized industries should not have left the monopolies intact, but that the opportunity should have been taken to break them down into separate and smaller businesses.

If the scandals associated with contested take-over bids continue, there is little doubt that far tougher standards will have to be laid down. Once the danger of contested take-overs is limited by law, then even agreed mergers will die down too, since a large proportion of them are purely defensive.

That may still leave too many small companies, which will have an increasing proportion of the national workforce, in the power of a few big merchant companies which dominate the market, just as fewer and fewer supermarket chains dominate their supplying industry. Americans have the answer in theory, but not apparently in practice. Their Robinson Patman Act aims to protect the small company against market domination by the large. But in the absence of really tough anti-trust laws, enforcing dominant corporations to divest themselves of parts of their business, Robinson Patman does not seem to be very effective. Even large sovereign governments seem to have been nervous of offending large and dominant corporations.

The political mood is changing. As big corporations divest themselves of their workforce, they divest themselves of voters. The big corporation is electorally friendless. It is well known that multi-nationals are too nervous to contribute to one political party. Even large national companies, who have to show such political contributions on their annual statements, are increasingly nervous about them. The disappearance of many big companies, household names for years, shows how friendless they have become. Once the public come to believe that they are no longer the source of jobs and that they are the major factor in the destabilizing condition of cost-push inflation, there will be a searching examination of their accumulation of economic power. Whatever is not fully justified will be split into units on a scale which is more human and more economically and socially benign. The European centre-right parties insist that they are not the representatives of big business, but of the small and medium-sized enterprise. Fairly soon they will have to show that that is true.

# The diffusion of economic power

Just as the Christians of the seventeenth century decided that the application of Christian doctrine to the political structure demanded the diffusion of political power, so I believe that the Christians of today will see that the application of Christian doctrine to the economic structure demands the diffusion of economic power.

There may be other ways of creating more employment. Many of us believe that the removal of the remaining major barriers to trade within the European Community will set in motion the great flywheel of inter-community trade and get many people back to work again. We also believe that there is a great deal of merit in the European Monetary System and the discipline of a stable currency with lower interest rates. And there is a great deal to be said for a concerted economic policy, which might enable us to raise growth rates by half of one per cent more a year. But when the two most vigorous economies of the Community, the German Federal Republic and the United Kingdom run into 'overheating', and may have to slow down when 17 million are unemployed, it becomes clear that something more is needed.

All the present evidence seems to point to the need for a major structural shift towards smaller companies and smaller plants, to point to the need for industry on a human scale. Easy access to work must be a Christian priority. The more doors there are, the more one of them is likely to be found open.

All my experience tells me that a diffusion of economic power is far more likely to come through a Conservative government than a socialist one. When I first joined the Conservative Party in 1946, the first Labour government to enjoy an overall majority was busy concentrating economic power into its own hands, both through a continuation of wartime controls into peacetime, and through the nationalization of key industries.

The Labour governments of the 1960s were content, after the failure of the National Plan, to use the National Economic Development Council, set up by the Macmillan government for voluntary indicative planning. But in the 70s, Labour tried to move back to centralized control. The top bracket of personal taxes went up to 98%, and capital transfer tax eventually took the bulk of undistributed profits. This was extremely discouraging for family-controlled businesses. Indeed many of them took it as a clear signal that government would prefer that they sold out to big business rather than expand and flourish under family control. One key Labour Cabinet minister told me that it was far easier for him to deal with big business than a multitide of small ones.

In economic management too the 70s were a time when, through the National Enterprise Board and industry planning agreements, the Labour government tried to add to its central control over prices and incomes. That was the time when I decided to go into politics.

The need is not for government control over the means of production, distribution and exchange, but for government to set the rules under which a market economy operates – including strong rules against accumulation and exploitation of private power. It was a Conservative Prime Minister who complained about the 'unacceptable face of capitalism'.

# Response to Sir Fred Catherwood and Pete Broadbent

*Francis Bridger*

## To Sir Fred Catherwood

I have two major, and a number of minor, observations about Sir Fred Catherwood's essay: the first cluster of observations is political, the second theological. My main political observation is that it is hard to recognize in this essay very much of contemporary Conservatism as practised during the Thatcher years. It may be true that *Sir Fred* regards full employment as the primary goal of governments, but that can hardly be said of the Thatcher administrations. Sir Geoffrey Howe's 1981 budget made a deliberate and calculated choice to put the control of inflation before the goal of full employment. The use of strict monetary policy to control monetary aggregates made it clear that this was so. Of course, much reference was made at the time to Jim Callaghan's dictum that inflation was both the mother and father of unemployment as a justification for rejecting the post-war consensus to which Sir Fred refers. In effect, however, the Conservatives chose to relegate the goal of full employment to second place.

A related political point I would want to make is that although Sir Fred's compassionate Conservatism is evident in his own approach, his brand of Toryism is light years away from the ideology of Thatcherism and the New Right. Another way of putting this is to say that Sir Fred is not representative of the mainstream of Conservative thinking and policy since 1979, where the emphasis has been upon economic efficiency rather than social welfare. One has only to look at the effects of market-oriented taxation, housing and social security policies to see that Conservatism, as embodied in actual legislation, is far from compassionate. As a local councillor responsible for implementing many of the so-called reforms in these areas, I know that Sir Fred's views are simply not reflected in the real political world. Social Toryism has all but collapsed (witness the departure of longstanding Cabinet 'wets' throughout 1980–90), though it will be interesting to see whether this strand of Conservatism undergoes a revival in the next few post-Thatcher years.

The unrepresentativeness of Sir Fred's Toryism is nowhere better shown than in his categorical rejection of monetarism which, despite the Lawson years, proved a constant theme in Prime Minister Thatcher's economic thinking. Similarly, Sir Fred's endorsement of fair wages, incomes policy, and trade unionism flies in the face of Mrs Thatcher's most basic instincts, not to mention her legislation. After all, how can these be reconciled with the ideology of free markets? There is a fundamental contradiction.

So, while I find myself in sympathy with much of what he says, I am not persuaded that Sir Fred's version of Conservatism is much more than wishful thinking.

On the theological side, I found his essay disappointing. The Bible and Christian theology are not allowed to critique contemporary Conservatism (as they must critique all political beliefs and parties). Indeed, the critical questions are not raised. Moreover, Sir Fred's discussion of Christian principles omits much important Old and New Testament material on attitudes to wealth, and care for the weak and vulnerable. It is simply untrue to suggest that the only picture of economic life we have in the Old Testament is idealized. As Chris Wright has shown, the land formed the basis of Israel's economic and social structures (at least until the time of the eighth-century prophets) such that the levitical laws were designed to ensure a system by which every family had access to means of production. Those who found themselves disadvantaged through ill fortune or exploitation were to be protected by (among other things) the Jubilee legislation.[1] So what we have in the Old Testament is a complex approach to economic and social well-being which is far from idealized.

When we turn to the New Testament, we are not faced with similar social legislation because the people of God are no longer understood as a geographically defined nation. What we do find, however, is a series of principles of justice and love which are continuous with the Old Testament.

The upshot of all this (as I have tried to show in my own essay) is that a careful consideration of biblical teaching suggests that both the policies and ideology of Conservatism are directly at variance with biblical principles of community, *agapē* and social justice.

# To Pete Broadbent

The points at which I take issue with Pete Broadbent are less theological (with one significant exception) than political. Let me begin with the theological.

Pete's exposition of the relationship between principles of justice and love is similar to my own and so I shall simply say that we are in substantial agreement. I do have misgivings, however, about what he means in his section *Some underlying assumptions* when he speaks of God as 'a God whose future is the ultimate destiny of the universe', and again, 'a God of paradox, both unchanging and with change as his very nature.'

I presume this derives from the German theologians Wolfhart Pannenberg and Jurgen Moltmann. Certainly the language is that of historicism (which has been criticized in depth by Oliver O'Donovan[2]). The problem is that in the context of this essay it is highly problematic. In what sense is God 'the future of the universe'? The apostle Paul's analysis in Colossians 1:15–20 is not that the future of God (whatever that means) is to be understood as identical with the universe, but that all creation will find its completion in Jesus Christ as the one by whom all things were created, and in whom all things are held together.

Equally, what sense (if any) does it make to speak of God as possessing unchanging attributes, and at the same time being subject to change? There is a deep theological controversy, not to say a philosophical and logical problem, here. For if God is subject to change, what kind of change? And what evidence from Scripture exists to show that this is the case?

Moreover, if God does change, is this the result of outside influence or does it arise from within his own being? If the former, then God becomes subject to someone else's control and he ceases to be supreme. If the latter, what is it within himself that gives rise to such change?

These could reasonably be regarded as abstruse theological questions if it were not for the political implications Pete seeks to draw from them. For, following a standard historicist line, he argues from this understanding of God to a political approach in which the present and the past are diminished in favour of the future. At the political level, this seems to me to be disastrous. The status quo may be highly questionable at key points, but we are not free to ignore our history, or to write it off as if it were wholly bad. More ironically, of course, the rejection of tradition and the assumption that we must look only to the future for values is precisely the mind-set of Mrs Thatcher and the New Right. They assume that in order to build a better world, we must begin not with human beings as they find themselves within given historical narratives, but with an intellectually constructed blueprint of what seems rationally desirable. Both Pete's theology and Mrs Thatcher's ideology converge at this point.

Theologically, such an approach is questionable both because it devalues history as the place where God has acted, and because it abandons the doctrine of the continuity of creation with redemption in favour of an over-emphasis on a future which will be discontinuous with what has gone before.

This leads me to my political criticism. In the second half of his essay, Pete devotes considerable space to a critique of Gladstonian liberalism in the erroneous view that this is the only tradition that liberalism has ever possessed. If it were, then his strictures against individualism would carry considerable weight.

However, he seems not to be aware of that strand of liberalism flowing from T. H. Green rather than J. S. Mill which I have termed 'communitarian liberalism'. I shall not discuss this here since I have gone into some detail in my essay. Suffice it to say that the Aunt Sally at which Pete tilts is not the philosophy of the Liberal Democratic Party as I have made clear. Gladstonian liberalism is alive and thriving in the New Right, as he identifies, but it has little part to play in modern Liberal Democratic philosophy.

One final point. I find myself in agreement with many of Pete's views but is he any more representative of the real Labour Party than Fred Catherwood is of the Conservatives? Both of them seem closer to Liberal Democracy than they appear to recognize.

# Response to Pete Broadbent and Francis Bridger

## Sir Fred Catherwood

I have read the contributions of Pete Broadbent and Francis Bridger with the greatest interest. In writing my own contribution, I had not thought that the book was to be quite so party-political. My view was, and still is, that it is more productive to look in some depth at a particular problem, to do a case-study related to the very real political problems confronting government, than to attribute all that goes wrong to the mistaken ideology of the other side.

So it is still not at all clear to me how either the Labour Party or the Liberal Democrats would tackle the problem of shop-floor power. This is contrary to all that the unions stand for, gives to those with bargaining power and takes from those who have not, including especially those who are thrown out of work in the process. My own solution is that we should diffuse economic power by deconcentration, just as we diffused political power through democracy.

Socialist policies have tended to concentrate power in the mistaken belief that it can be made democratically accountable. That is not the experience I have had in my years in public service, and the Labour Party has now backed down, though not to the extent of removing Clause 4. But the emphasis on ideology in Pete Broadbent's paper worries me. A Christian already has an ideology and I don't think we have need of any other. I find myself much more in agreement with the relation between faith and politics in Francis Bridger's paper.

I have, for instance, great difficulty with the primacy given to equality in Pete Broadbent's paper. Of course I agree that the law that all property should revert to families every fifty years did promote equality in Israel (so far as it was ever implemented). That is why I support a rate of death duties which has the effect of redistributing capital every second generation.

Labour policy has, however, gone much further than that. In the mid-1970s I visited a very successful export company in Consett, employing 200 people. I asked the owner why, since he was doing so well, he did not double the company and double his exports. He said that the Labour government clearly did not want him to do so. There were risks in taking on 200 untried people. If he were successful, government left him only 2% of the profit, and if he failed, he damaged all he had. I couldn't budge him. Consett could have done with the extra jobs and so could a lot of other places where the effect of marginal taxes at 98% was the same.

By contrast, the lowering of marginal taxes by the Conservatives has promoted the growth of hundreds of small companies in new industries and given employment to hundreds of thousands. It has not solved the problem of unemployment, but it has certainly made it a lot easier than it was a few years ago. I know that that makes a lot of people very much richer than the average; but it seems to me that if, to prevent that, we have to discourage those who want to invest and give employment, we are cutting off our noses to spite our face and, in any case in fifty years, capital taxes will have taken their toll.

I also notice with great interest that neither Pete Broadbent nor Francis Bridger attack the Conservative Party. They concentrate their fire entirely on the 'New Right'.

Indeed Pete Broadbent, in his response, distinguishes the 'New Right' from 'Conservatism'. Having read what he says about the 'New Right', I am content to remain a 'Conservative'. I also notice that he says that the New Right are in the old liberal tradition and that Francis Bridger repudiates that tradition. So I am strongly reinforced in my view that it is better in the pragmatic tradition of Conservatism to concentrate, as I have done, on a central problem, and see whether a Conservative can come up with an answer which is within that tradition.

# Response to Fred Catherwood and Francis Bridger

*Pete Broadbent*

Despite the fact that the three writers in this section started with an identical brief, it is apparent that we have all interpreted it very differently! It has therefore proved difficult to engage with all that my fellow contributors have written. I share Francis Bridger's misgivings about attempting to derive biblical principles from particular scriptural texts. It will have been obvious from my own contribution that I do not believe that it is really possible to develop a political theology by using this particular methodology. Perhaps this is why Fred Catherwood is able to write that he finds 'no problem in agreeing all the objectives set out in the first set of propositions'! I hope that readers of this volume will be encouraged to go beyond the 'proof-texting' approach which both Francis and I find inadequate.

## Conservatism – but which brand?

My biggest problem with Fred Catherwood's contribution is that it simply does not represent the reality of Conser-

vative political philosophy as it now is. Fred's benevolent paternalism would be dismissed by New Right
ideologues, who would not assent to his proposition that
there is a consensus that 'the state should be responsible
for social security'. Nor does the concept of free collective
bargaining which he describes at the beginning of his
chapter find favour in contemporary Conservative circles.

Fred bases his approach on a commitment to a policy of
full employment. In doing so, he ignores some of the
questions about the nature of work which I raise in my
chapter, and appears to equate 'work' with paid employment. Employment does not seem to be the most obvious
policy area over which Christians will agree, and I wonder
whether, underlying Fred's contribution, there is a hidden
assumption that the Protestant work ethic is an expression
of the biblical understanding of work and employment (an
assumption which I would question).

His exposition of the 'small is beautiful' approach to
economics is attractive, but there is little evidence that the
free market will allow the evolution of SMEs (small and
medium-sized enterprises) to continue if their existence
begins to challenge the concentration of power in monopoly capitalist corporations. The market does not, by
definition, regulate itself in order to move towards a particular organizational pattern. It seems inevitable that
state intervention will be required in order to bring about
the major structural shift towards smaller companies that
Fred advocates.

# Freedom and ideological suspicion

Francis Bridger and I are at one in our distaste both for the
atomistic liberalism of J. S. Mill, and for the political
outworking of that philosophy in contemporary Conservatism. We have both argued strongly for the corporate
'strand' in biblical theology. What Francis calls 'communitarian liberalism' seems at first sight not very different from the democratic socialism for which I have
argued in my chapter. Francis seems obsessed with the

idea that socialism is of necessity bureaucratic, reliant on the power of the state, and denies the importance of the individual. In my own chapter, I referred to the concept of 'ideological suspicion' which liberation theologians have employed as a methodology for criticizing western theology. It is interesting to see Francis using that same methodology in his evaluation of the Labour Party. His 'second reading' of what he calls Labour revisionism is that the Labour Party has not really changed its policies, and that it is, at heart, still only a party of collectivism. Whatever the Labour Party says it stands for, Francis reserves the right to believe that it really stands somewhere else! Of course, politicians do not find it easy to credit their opponents with a change of mind or heart – but perhaps there is a need for us to be more generous, and actually listen to each other! (Which probably means that my comments in the next paragraph should be read in the same light . . .)

The choice for Christians who cannot support Conservatism is not an easy one. On the one hand lies a liberalism which, if it can truly shake off its individualistic past, can claim to hold together the Christian belief in the importance of the individual with a vision of the interdependence of persons. On the other hand, there is a socialism which claims to have moved away from imposed collectivist solutions to embrace a philosophy in which the individual and the collective are held together in the pursuit of equality and justice.

My reservations about the liberal/centre position are these:

1. Is there not a danger that the rejection of collectivism fails to follow through to a logical conclusion the organic metaphors which Scripture uses to describe life in the church and in society? (See, for example, Francis' exposition of the body of Christ metaphor.) Liberalism, spawned in individualism, seems incapable of shaking off that very western understanding of human beings in community which denies the reality of solidarity when solidarity begins to express itself in terms of class or race consciousness.

2. Liberal thinkers seem, secondly, strangely naive about the structures of power and oppression in our society, and I would want to question whether 'communitarian liberalism' would begin to deal with some of the root injustices in the distribution of wealth, availability of resources, and equality of opportunity which socialists have identified and focused on.

3. Finally, liberals need to face the uncomfortable fact that, for all that they disown the individualistic nineteenth-century liberalism which spawned the New Right, it is the rock from which they were hewn. The communal emphasis in politics is something which the Labour Party has always promoted, and, despite Francis Bridger's theological framework, with which I am in almost complete agreement, there is a suspicion that the foundations on which liberalism is built cannot really bear the weight of their new-found communitarianism.

Although there is much that divides us, we are united as Christians in our belief that the policies of the last decade have had appalling consequences for our people and our country. The opportunity for Christians to rid themselves of the cancer of Conservatism will come at the next election. Perhaps our exploration of the alternatives will have helped in that process.

# Part 3

## Views from outside: Independent assessments of the main parties

### Alan Storkey
### Philip Giddings

*To what extent do you think that the views of the role of the state in economic life and welfare provision held by each of the main parties reflect the biblical principles contained in theses 7–19 (and any additional ones you consider to be of central relevance)? What implications would you draw from your conclusions regarding Christian participation in these parties?*

# Economic policy and the Welfare State

*Alan Storkey*

> The Conservative Party ● The independent and
> the dependent ● Wealth creation ● Money,
> finance and capital ● Self-interest, property
> and justice ● The Labour Party ● Politicized
> economic life ● The public and the private ●
> Finance and capitalism ● The Welfare State ●
> The Liberal Democrats ● Functionalism or
> citizenship? ● Radical individualism ● Con-
> clusion.

Do the main political parties reflect a Christian perception
of economic life and the Welfare State? And how do we
approach this question? We could bring a shopping list of
requirements against which we evaluate the performance
of each of the parties. But this judgment would require
some complex justification. For example, is the state
retirement pension too low or too high? Most parties
would like, in principle, to push the pension higher, but
there are other priorities. It therefore becomes very
difficult to judge specific policies in isolation. In this

paper I should therefore like to adopt a different approach. The emphasis will be on uncovering the underlying frameworks with which each party approaches these issues so as to evaluate them in terms of the Christian principles discussed in this book.

One problem which all politicians face is the disjunction between the rhetoric and policies on the one hand and the reality and practices on the other. Thus, for example, successive governments in Britain have declared that they are primarily concerned with turning the economy round through some set of policies which are deemed to be the necessary prerequisite. By most lights those governments have failed, and therefore what they have actually been doing is different from what has been claimed. Every political situation seems more complicated than we say and is only partly articulated. Indeed, one of the most astonishing facts about economic life is the way unintended consequences continue to roll off events and surprise us. In this area especially, therefore, what is may not be what is said. It may seem that this is just a prelude to accusing each of the parties of hypocrisy. In a sense it is, but only because hypocrisy and illusion is the problem we all face in our political responses. Things are not much different from when the false prophets said 'Peace, peace' inaccurately. We are all false in our own way, and it is therefore important to try to look at what is the case as well as what is said to be the case. This does not mean that Christians are any less fallible, but our Book holds words and deeds up to examination, and so must we.

So in this study I shall not necessarily describe the views of the main parties in the way they describe themselves, although that freedom may lead us no closer to the truth; the reader will judge whether or not that is the case. What, then, are the perspectives of each party on economic life and welfare provision?

# The Conservative Party

## The independent and the dependent

In the 1983 Conservative manifesto Margaret Thatcher spoke thus about the Welfare State:

> We have a duty to protect the most vulnerable members of our society, many of whom contributed to the heritage we now enjoy. We are proud of the way we have shielded the pensioner and the National Health Service from the recession. Only if we create wealth can we continue to do justice to the old and the sick and the disabled. It is economic success which will provide the surest guarantee of help for those who need it most.

This theme of the independent and the dependent has been important in Conservative philosophy. The underlying conception is of dependent groups who are being supported by those who are able to support themselves. The membership of the two groups may change, but the ratio between them is crucial. The higher the independent /dependent ratio, the easier is welfare provision. Nor is it just a question of welfare, for there is also a trickle-down effect which means that the wealth of the independent naturally moves down to those who were previously dependent. Obviously, the aim of welfare within this perspective is to move people from the dependent to the independent sector, to 'help them stand on their own two feet'. Although there are those, like the sick and disabled, who will always need help, private health insurance and other forms of self-help can obviate even these needs.

The basic question is whether or not this is a biblical model of things. It can be argued that it is not, on two counts. Firstly, the biblical commitment to independence is far stronger than the Conservative one. Being independent in terms of livelihood, family, before the law and within the nation and community, is in biblical terms not a matter of *laissez-faire*, but of corporate commitment. It involves the transfer of resources and wealth, so that no person may look down on his or her neighbour, on a regular basis. Freedom from economic slavery, and to economic stewardship and responsibility, was a norm requiring commitment and action, not a supposed automatic process. In order to become independent those who are poor and dependent need good education, job training, a transfer of wealth from those who have a lot, forms of welfare which allow the exercise of responsibility, ways of controlling credit and debt and the availability of jobs. Rather than reflecting this commitment to the dependents, Conservatives have tended to move resources away from the poor through taxation, child benefit, regional, educational and social security policy, and have reallocated it towards the rich through interest rate, credit, trade and industrial policy.

My conclusion is that the commitment to independence is a nominal one in relation to those who are poor, without resources and presently dependent. Rather than take seriously the process of helping them to move through to independence, there is a shoulder-shrugging attitude to those who are seen as a resourceless underclass – those without a job, who don't own their own house and shares, and who cannot make ends meet. The principle of independence seems only to apply to those who already have it. Indeed, many in these groups, through lower taxes, windfall profits from the sale of public sector corporations, pension and share purchase incentives, high mortgage tax relief, the introduction of the poll tax and other handouts to those who are affluent, have been far more dependent on state benefits than the poor. In actual practice, over the last decade, it is the rich who have been dependent on the state, the opposite of what is conveyed by the independent/dependent myth (theses 11 and 15).

But there is another view of the issue. As well as the biblical emphasis on distributing resources so that all can exercise economic stewardship before God independently, the Bible shows we are all servants of one another, and mutually dependent. No member of the community can claim not to depend on others. Given this interdependence, the fairness of the transactions which take place between those who are mutually interdependent is crucial; they must love their neighbours as themselves, and must not claim an autonomy which is not theirs. Often those who most claim independence have been given most by earlier generations, the educational system, their companies and communities.

## Wealth creation

Another major theme of Conservative economic philosophy in the last decade is the idea of wealth creation. It is allied to the previous principle, because independent people are seen as those who are capable of adding value to goods and services to make more wealth.[1] This wealth is the source of the taxable income which can then be appropriated to the welfare services. The standard of welfare provision is thus seen as being based on the wealth generated in the economy privately. The process of wealth creation is usually identified with private business, and especially with the entrepreneurial decision-maker.[2] The last decade has been hailed as the era of the triumph of business and capitalism. The collapse of the Eastern European and Soviet economic system has largely been interpreted as the triumph of wealth-creating capitalism, and is seen as the final verification of this way of seeing economics. The idea of wealth creation has now assumed unreal and magical qualities in addition to the misconceptions on which it is based.

This can be seen by looking more soberly at the two countries which are seen as exemplifying most fully this wealth-creating ideal, Germany and Japan. Since 1945 these countries have devoted negligible resources to military expenditure, while their major world rivals, the former USSR, the United States, Britain, France and other countries have been spending up to 5% of their GNP on military expenditure. The difference of, say, 3% compound over the 45 years since the war is an awful lot of GNP, enough to explain most of the difference in economic development which has occurred in that period, especially when cumulative advantages are taken into account. Indeed, the relative economic weakness of the former USSR with its limited resource base, and the United States, with its massive post-war advantages, can also be similarly described. It is partly the economic pressure of this waste of resources which has brought about the great disengagement of East-West confrontation. A substantial part of the German and Japanese wealth-creating 'miracles' arise merely from not locking up resources in missile silos, tanks and aircraft carriers.

The basic misconception is the failure to recognize the qualitative difference between two things. One is our dependence on God's creative provision of all the resources which we use in our economic life. The other is human activity which merely stewards and develops these resources. A less important one is the identification of wealth creation with production, business and finance. It is clear that families, the state, communities, voluntary agencies, public corporations, schools and colleges, hospitals and arts groups are able to add value, not just private sector enterprises. Similarly, it is also clear that the latter through lavish offices, expense account accommodation and meals, company cars, pollution-generation, stress-related illness, and forms of consumer addiction, are eating and destroying wealth on a massive scale. All economic agents are therefore accountable for the value and resources which they develop, or use up and destroy. There is no serious justification for a magical identification of value development with private companies and entrepreneurs.

Allied with these misconceptions has been a failure in the last decade to develop solid British value-added output which will be of use in the rest of the world. The (temporary) cushion of North Sea oil has allowed the British to ignore how deeply they are dependent on overseas production. Import penetration is so deep in most industries that it is now difficult to see any strong domestic, let alone export, production base being established. Much of the 'wealth creation' of the last decade has consisted of property, share and market value speculation, which is later eroded as value-loss. Here again, the explicit policy emphasis turns out other than it seems.

## Money, finance and capital

Underlying the economic vision of wealth creation is a basic inconsistency which faces us all, but which Conservatism especially enters. The basic argument is that money measures, through national income, the growth and improvement in the economy; that profitability measures the working success of companies; and that what happens on the Stock Exchange measures the capital values of companies. The last ten years especially have seen the development of the financial sector as the authoritative way of establishing economic policy and direction. The City has provided the economic direction for Conservatism. Although monetarism was initially a movement for re-establishing a stable price level through exercising tight control on the money supply, behind the policy commitment lies a belief that money accounting is the unequivocal basis for private and public economic policy. Thus the process of encouraging hospitals to move into self-governing accounting is an example of the extension of this principle.

One problem with this position on money accounting is the way it fails to take into account user costs, externalities, pollution and social costs. A large increase in GNP can now merely be new patterns of expenditure which are necessary to meet pollution problems, protect families against encroachments on their lifestyle which they do not like, or respond to slower traffic. Higher accounting values can therefore reflect increased social costs rather than higher welfare. A second problem is that variations in market prices often lead to drastic changes in what are claimed as the real value of assets. A new and growing group of people now make a living from juggling asset values in increasingly unstable markets. Somehow this is seen as a decisive activity; take-over bids, asset stripping, mergers and management buy-outs are seen as the sharp end of economic development, rather than as the by-product of unstable market structures. A third problem with this position is the way it refuses to take into account the extent to which many market prices are unfair, especially when some groups have so little money that they can be exploited or their wishes count for nought. A fourth problem is that many purchases are of things which are bad, addictive or represent subverted values. Of course, people have to be free to make some of these poor choices, but that is no reason for trusting these valuations themselves.

All of these problems are, however, unimportant beside the underlying fallacy. It is human valuation which is reflected, for good or bad, in money prices. The valuation of resources, work, usefulness, worth, quality, purpose and human costs enters into, and defines, all the prices which occur throughout a market system. These valuations must take into account existing prices, but they also shape them. We make markets; they are the work of our hands and reflect our values and decisions. If, rather than making these valuations, we bow down before the work of our own hands, and ask it to make our decisions and valuations for us, we are worshipping a broken idol which will mock us with its foolishness. Yet this is what is happening within Conservative philosophy. We will find when the market is asked to tell us what is good health care, transport policy, education, military expenditure, community development and family welfare policy that we get out the same garbled valuations as are put in. Precisely because responsibility has not been taken for real values and decisions, most developments happen by default and haphazardly. Only when responsibility is undertaken in accounting and pricing for this valuation can a sober use of money develop.

## Self-interest, property and justice

Another fundamental tenet of Conservative economic philosophy is its individualism, which is reflected in the idea that rights of ownership and property are absolute. This in turn is related to a self-referencing view of economic decisions and purchasing. Each individual is lord of his or her economic domain, is independent (in the sense of the first theme discussed above), and looks to his or her own satisfaction in work, leisure, consumption and investment. This is the mainspring of economic activity, and is its end. In practical terms, of course, this has meant a concentration during this decade on consumption, leisure, homes and holidays. It has been accompanied by very high levels of consumer credit and imports, low levels of saving, and high interest rates. This era will probably be seen in the future as the one which above all, was concerned with instant gratification, and gave the lowest priority to later generations. Conservatism, supporting the absolute rights of property and ownership, has effectively eliminated all wealth taxes and redistributive ones; local authority rates have been the latest to go. Ownership is nine tenths of the law.

Along with this individualism goes a sense of individual worth: rewards correspond with desert, and justify the position of the wealthy and propertied. Risk, astuteness, striving, or a sense of superiority validate whatever patterns of accumulation of wealth, economic power and property exist. Correspondingly, the less deserving are just that. This, of course, does not correspond with reality. Those who have a lot find it relatively easy to make more. Often market fluctuations, legacies, luck, fortuitously taking part in an expanding market, monopoly power or scarcity value have more to do with high rewards than any moral sense of desert. Many of the poor also work very hard under more difficult conditions.

The deeper problem with this position is that developing value is an interdependent process. It is not possible to divorce the decision of the managing director from the contribution of the workers who implement it, or the success of farmers from the prices that are set by the Common Agricultural Policy. Thus, the Personal Equity Plans introduced by the Conservative government in January 1987 are channelling something like 2 billion pounds into the Stock Market annually. City brokers are not exclusively responsible for the extra rewards which come their way as a result of this change. This myth of justified reward has isolated the 'successful' in the southeast and elsewhere from the recognition that many Welfare State policy decisions may be partisan and unfair in their bias towards the affluent. Thus, when income tax exemption for large mortgages is retained alongside market level council house rents, it smells of special pleading. Or when the doctrine of independent financial accountability is waived for student grants, commuter trains and Covent Garden Opera House it suggests less than evenhandedness. My conclusion is that the myth of self-reward is not only untrue, but is also a justification for ignoring claims which other members of the community rightly have.

Here is another important biblical theme: the poor and the weak can be easily wronged, and their case needs to be given due weight. The Conservative doctrine of automaticity, and the proper desert of the affluent, rules out consideration of whether the poor have been wronged. Often workers who have helped build up good companies in one area have seen capital and jobs shipped overseas. The sale of public assets has shifted more than a billion pounds in windfall gains and fees to the pockets of the affluent. The noise and pollution of the transport of the rich by plane and car is dumped largely on the poor. Rich suburbanites, while quite happy to use inner city facilities, seem unworried by the fact that teachers and education are not available for children in these areas in denial of statutory requirements. The poll tax, other tax rates and allowances have often meant that low income families are paying a higher proportion of their income in taxes than high income earners. Areas in Docklands for wealthy groups receive far greater incentives and grants than those which house the poor. Prosperous companies receive massive handouts of dubious legality, while poor areas struggle for basic loans. These are questions of interpersonal and intergroup justice which tend not to be heard within a framework which is concerned only with self-interested individuals and things.

These beliefs and attitudes, it seems to me, strongly inhibit the infusion of Christian perceptions into the Conservative Party. They are travelling in a different direction from Christian understanding and are generating contradictions and weaknesses which are serious. Of course, various emphases wax and wane with the changing personnel and commitment of the party. We have not looked in detail at welfare policies occurring at a particular time. Sometimes they are responding to electoral or media pressure and are, in part, better than the overall philosophy. Yet the faith in wealth, independence, finance and property has had a pervasive influence, and without holding it up to question we cannot see why what is said and what happens differ so fundamentally. At root 1990s Conservatism does not seem able to respond obediently to biblical norms of welfare and care, because the heart of the party is elsewhere; it believes in automatic material progress, and those who are the vehicle of its implementation. This faith fails to address the reality which faces us in Britain today, and is generating more and more mythical interpretations of the British economy.

# The Labour Party

The Labour Party has traditionally been seen as the party of the working class, and of those who are economically weak. Surely this means that it meets the kind of ethical criteria set out in the opening theses – emphasizing resources for the poor, welfare, the right to work and a fair wage. On these grounds Lord Soper and a long tradition of other Christians have claimed that it is scarcely possible for a Christian to be other than a socialist. In the analysis which follows this presumption will be questioned, but not so much on ethical grounds as in terms of its whole conception of economic life and welfare.

## Politicized economic life

One of the biggest puzzles of modern western politics is how a movement started in earnest by Karl Marx proclaiming the withering away of the state could have developed into such a state-centred ideology. Marx was very different from his successors. He spent years poring over the economic theories of Ricardo, Malthus and Mill and saw the structure of economic life as basic to existence, while they (Lenin, Trotsky, Bukharin, Luxemburg, the Webbs and others) moved over to a much more politicized view of economics, and even proclaimed the withering away of political economy. Why did this happen? The answer is, I think, still fundamental to the question of where the Labour Party stands today.[3]

Initially Marx lived in a *laissez-faire* era when there was a minimal state, and getting a means of living was the central issue of life for most people. His conception was of economics falling apart as a result of its inner contradictions and certain inevitable processes of development. This view, although it took economics very seriously, saw it as essentially negative, a process which in the form of capitalism was doomed to destruction. Although at the time this was the most powerful economic critique, it lacked real penetrating power because its judgments were sweeping and dogmatic, rather than being specific to what actually was wrong in economic life. Changes in technology, education, union activity and principles of justice in employment had their impact on the working class and prevented Marx's prophesied lumpenproletariat from emerging.

This old-style Marxism was overtaken by a new political philosophy just at the time when the Labour Party was being formed. It had its origin in German political philosophy and national life, and it involved a fundamental belief in the state as the source of identity of the nation and the unit which could mobilize national economic life. In my view the modern Labour Party has never realized how decisively its approach has been influenced by the German statist tradition. Marx, of course, shaped his own early ideas in reaction to the Hegelian versions of this tradition, and much of his later economic work has a more liberal British context. He was not much read, and was of limited influence in the early Labour Party, compared with the Fabian and other reformist groups. These looked more strongly to Bismarckian Germany, and its development of a paternalist Welfare State as the model which socialists could adopt. By this time T. H. Green, Bernard Bosanquet and the other English Idealist philosophers had introduced a systemic view of political philosophy to the intelligensia, and nationalistic rivalry had replaced liberalism as the strongest public motive in politics. On this view the state became the embodiment of the nation, the source of progress, the focus of goodness, the inclusive institution, and the will of the majority working class. The latter theme was the locus of many valuable reforms, but this was despite the woolly and potentially dangerous philosophy of the state which was caught up with it, and which the Labour Party largely espoused.

The Marxist vision of one economic order being replaced by another was superseded by the state-directed political order for economic life. In Russia it was of a centralized command economy dictated by the Communist Party. In Britain a number of more democratic models have taken shape within this vision: nationalizing the commanding industries of the economy for reasons of equity and efficiency, the central indicative planning of wartime and George Brown's Department of Economic Affairs, the macro-economic Keynesian managed economy, the consultative planning of the 60s and 70s, and, more recently, a state partnership model which depends also on German and French models of National Corporatism. Here the state sees itself as the partner in the development and success of its own national industries in the international competition which they face. The point here is to note the underlying conception of state involvement in economic life which all these forms have in common, even when, as recently, they are diluted by a stronger commitment to private economic activity.

Behind all of them is a conception of daily economic activity as vaguely anarchic and potentially destructive. Because economics *per se* is not healthy, it needs to be rescued by the state in some way or another, either to establish justice, or increase efficiency, or sort out disorder. The mode in which the state engages with the economy is primarily one of participation, either by control, or more recently by consultation. The criticism of this position is its failure to recognize the integrity and character of economic transactions in their own terms. To put it another way, the advisers in Whitehall (or Brussels) cannot and should not suggest to industrialists, bankers and retailers how to run their businesses. To put it in more sinister terms, there is a long European history of totalitarianism in Germany, Italy, Russia and other countries (of both right and left) which involves state control and direction of industry. Despite the good intentions of many participants in these forms of socialist economic vision, there is something basically flawed in this underlying perspective.

In biblical terms the error is that of replacing God's rule in the lives of people with a political reference point. The state is seen as a source of economic salvation, of order, of direction for economic life which it cannot really fulfil. Nor can it really reflect the deeper and fuller meanings of economic life and decision-making in the lives of citizens. This is because its blanket negativity means that the perspective is unable to discern good, and destructive, patterns of economic life in relation to God's norms for stewardship and blessing. Consequently, the state's plan always turns out to be shallow and controlling. Ironically, the ideology which first developed the concept of alienated work in relation to capitalism, and rightly so, has now also produced on a massive scale, work alienation in relation to the state which was exposed in the upheavals of Eastern Europe. At the same time this conception of state direction means that the biblical, limited, defining function of the state – which is to establish lawful and just relationships – has often not been undertaken. Justice in the distribution of wealth, capital, education and technology, fairness in markets, companies, banking and indebtedness and right work, have not been addressed by socialist economic policy, other than in terms of political take-over. The old polarization of self-interest or state control has left the just structuring of economic relationships, markets and institutions underdeveloped.

## The public and the private

This orientation has led to a similar reactive attitude to public and private. The Labour Party, faced with the automatic Conservative adulation of private wealth, has tended to assert the value of public or nationalized wealth, and to believe in the inherent goodness of state use of funds, whether for welfare or other purposes. The tired debate goes on, locked in to the law of the excluded middle; wealth and resources have to be either public (state-controlled), or private. This is reflected in the nationalization, denationalization, renationalization debate which should have died decades back, but is given new life by Conservative policy on British Telecom, Gas, Water and anything else which brings in revenue. The problem all the time has been the failure of both sides, in the simplistic political debate which our voting system encourages, to recognize the proper categories of ownership. It is worth, at this stage, looking at a more biblical perspective on ownership, or more accurately stewardship. Only with this are we fully able to face the complexities of modern economic life.

Ownership which is seen in absolute, possessive terms is wrong. Land is being used by birds, worms, walkers, those who enjoy the view, and many others in a way which makes any ownership use partial. In the modern world with transport, mineral extraction, mobile resources, the ownership of education and technology, renting, borrowing and lending, the old idea of possessive ownership as an absolute right is even more untenable. The biblical perspective recognizes that stewardship or trust gives responsibilities of a proxy before God, who alone has absolute claims over that which he has created. Proximate ownership thus carries responsibilities of use, replenishment, care, nurture and development in relation to the natural resources which are temporarily entrusted to us, and also responsibilities to others who stand in relationships of neighbour, exchange, worker, consumer or provider. The Mosaic laws of fallow, gleaning, animal care, feasts, Sabbath, Jubilee, cancellation of debt and many others reflect these relations of trust and responsibility which are also matched, in even greater complexity, in our own economy. So-called 'private' ownership is really a set of relationships of trust and responsibility, of blessing and duty, which need to be fully acknowledged and understood. Many of our laws of 'private ownership' have failed to recognize this, and as a result we have pollution, environmental decay, under-used private facilities, public blight, over-exploitation and a lazy, leisured group of property owners who contribute little communally. The Labour reaction into 'state' ownership fails to recognize that the state bureaucrats, given use of this property, can also exploit it to their own ends, as has happened in Eastern Europe. Only when a more sensitive and proximate understanding of property is developed, and we break out of the public/private dichotomy, are the answers to a range of important questions going to be available. Conservatives will have to realize that the distribution of wealth and property is firmly on the agenda, and socialists that 'public' is far wider than state ownership.

## Finance and capitalism

Historically socialism has fought against the evils of capitalism, including the exploitation of labour, low wages, work impoverishment, colonial exploitation of resources and workers, and monopoly power. The responses to these problems generated the trade unions, policies of nationalization, employment legislation, and moves towards the independence of colonies. Yet partly because of its historic fixation on capitalism, and because of the adherence to a negative economic stance, it is now in a situation where it is not even addressing the questions which are on the economic agenda. One of the key ones, for example, is the disjunction between finance and industry. The CBI has repeatedly criticized what it has called 'short-termism', the way immediate short-term financial strategies seem to win out over longer-term industrial development. Alongside this problem is the failure of much of British industry and commerce to undertake long-term investment, research and development, so that it is being by-passed in terms of exports, product designs and technology. The Labour Party is thinking of this failure only in terms of state-induced regeneration of investment and training, not in terms of the structural relationship between finance and capital.[4]

Another important issue is the generation of pollution by the industrialist and consumer. Clearly, a response involves a change in the taxation pattern, so that, for example, the price of petrol rises 50% more or less immediately, and other items which have user or producer costs in terms of pollution are taxed more heavily. But this in turn involves industrial and consumer-oriented policies which address patterns of hardship. The long-term aim is a restructuring of production and consumption through price which curbs many of the indulgences of modern consumerism. Because this does not fit with the 'capitalist' problem, it is not an issue which can be addressed in socialist categories. The current policy statement does address the ecological problem, but without an awareness of the changes in accounting principle which relational economics involves.

Important, also, is the mobility of short-term finance and the way it can move quickly into share and other markets internationally. One of the consequences of this pattern is the extent to which markets are formed by speculative money, and the unstable price levels which many of these markets exhibit. Allied to this is the potential vulnerability of particular nations to flights or influxes of finance, which can far outweigh their trading imbalances, and of the world economy to such an unstable base. Obviously, this is a question which needs international consultation and co-operation, but because the Labour Party's position does not allow a normative analysis of productive and destructive market patterns in relation to the commodities and communities in which they operate, it has not developed an economic response on this issue either.[5]

Similarly, the exploitation of credit consumers by the

banks and other large finance companies belongs to another domain which does not neatly fit 'capitalist' analysis. In part the Labour Party has accepted the Conservative idea of unlimited freedom to get credit. Although at earlier periods public sector mortgages were more common, there has now been a fairly complete retreat from direct state involvement in lending, and as yet norms relating to the problem of usury have not been developed in Labour Party policy statements.

This general argument is subject to all kinds of qualifications, as there are groups that think through responses to economic issues and try to work out a better way forward. Yet still the Labour philosophy fails to engage in contemporary terms with good norms of economic activity, and with the evils which are generated in terms other than those which can be included under the label 'capitalism', especially through financial claims and liabilities. On reflection this seems not just a failure of policy, but also a far deeper failure to appreciate the biblical understanding of the nature of these claims and liabilities. They tend to be treated as items in themselves which are either a law to themselves and can operate freely in whatever markets are created, the Conservative view, or to be treated as inherently suspect by Labour as the title deeds of capitalism. Yet the terms on which titles, claims and liabilities are created involve living economic relationships among the participants which can be drastically, and often unfairly, changed by circumstances like inflation, exchange, interest and tax rates, market conditions and distributional factors. Christianity has always recognized the relativity of financial obligations, as Jesus' parable of forgiven debt shows. This requires the evaluation of financial claims in terms of the norms and proper relationships of the people, and the conditions which occur in particular situations. Thus the cancellation of debt, the revaluation of assets, changes in obligation, interest and transfer are already subject to revision, and must be in more principled terms than they are now.

## The Welfare State

The conception of welfare which has emerged in Labour thinking has historically been of state paternalism. Recently this has given way to an idea of partnership between the state and other agencies. The welfare conception which focuses on benefit payments, as rights conferred by the state on individuals, led to a pattern of dependency where the benevolence of the state was seen as the major force for good in British society. Many of the welfare provisions were good, and will seem increasingly valuable as a look-after-yourself mentality replaces them, but they led to an idea of control which never had the ambition of eliminating hardship, disability and lack of resources. It led to a passive dependence on the 'Council' or 'Social Security', which was also often an admission that real progress towards economic independence was not going to happen. Often the educational, technological, capital, family and infrastructure deprivation experienced by the poor and needy was, and is, underestimated. Sometimes, the stance was problem-perpetuating rather than remedial, especially because those running the Welfare State liked others to be beholden to it. Gradually the middle classes succeeded in getting welfare benefits travelling in their direction, and it became a question of political bargaining as to which political party could promise the best welfare package for the average citizen to win votes. Thus, the middle classes both undermined the principle of caring for the well-being of all, and then were fed and believed the idea that the Welfare State was not working.

The change in conception needed is to a state which is concerned with the loving justice which all citizens can expect from the wider community, and with a commitment to restore them, as far as is possible, from poverty and deprivation. It involves going the second mile to work for a remedy to poverty, sickness and economic weakness. At the same time communal welfare is far bigger than state provision. It involves family, church, voluntary organization, business, banking, education and the media. The 'state' must not therefore hijack to itself the notion of caring for the well-being of all, but encourage the good wherever it is found. Clearly the costs of this in terms of lower standards of consumption living may seen untenable at present, but the deeper costs in terms of broken families, poor educational standards, crime and social illness are also evident to most people.

The underlying argument of this section is that in both its economic policies, and its view of the Welfare State, the Labour Party does not at present have a viable ideological framework. Its commitment to the state as the organ of economic and welfare progress prevents it from getting to grips with the issues of justice and impoverishment which face the nation. The Christian awareness of the norms which direct all our economic and social relationships, and the specific tasks of justice associated with the state, are actually the way out of this ideological impasse. There are few signs, however, that this has yet been recognized. The Labour Party may get reactive moderate votes in Britain at the next election, but behind this lies the question of whether socialism offers the understanding of our political situation and a way forward. It does not seem to touch the deep issues which we now face.

# The Liberal Democrats

Undoubtedly the theme which comes most strongly from the Liberal Democrats is a repudiation of the axis which has dominated British politics for the first three quarters of this century. The law of the excluded middle which says you are either capitalist or socialist is no longer the logic of politics. This either/or is itself flawed and misstates many of our problems. Although the Liberal Democrats are also concerned with the polarity of our political institutions, this reaction is also reflected in their view of social and economic policy. How is it expressed? The kind of words which are important are partnership, community, sharing and participation. The focus is away from the state or the private individual, and towards the organization of industry, local government, education and community life. In view of the constraints imposed by the capitalist/Labour polarization on policy and political thinking, is this not a great step forward, and one which allows a greater freedom for Christian social and economic policy formation? First we must ask more fully what it means.

Politics abhors a vacuum, and parties cannot just be agnostic and wait for the mistakes of other parties to make them a more attractive alternative. Without vision the party perishes. The big question, therefore is in what name the Liberal Democratic Party repudiates the capitalist/Labour polarity, and here we must take note of both the Social Democrat and Liberal contributions.

## Functionalism or citizenship?

The Social Democrats' repudiation was done in the name of a conception of community. Its prior focus was 'social' as its name implied. This view has two streams of inspiration. One has its roots in the Fabian Society and a range of progressive social movements in the nineteenth and early twentieth centuries. The Fabians' economic policy espoused the utilitarian maxim of the greatest happiness of the greatest number, and saw the role of the state in terms of various forms of benevolent welfare. Interestingly, in their early days, the Fabians were quite happy to permeate the Liberal Party. This approach fits quite well with modern electoral politics. It involves making judgments about what will best benefit the community as a whole, and if a majority of the electorate agree, then the party gets elected.

However, appealing though this approach is, and well attuned with the new majority middle class, it could be argued that this Benthamite heritage is not only vague and muddled, but partakes of the moral bankruptcy which is part of contemporary humanist culture. What seems to make us happy is often a far cry from what is right or just. It is easy to look for what will keep the system ticking over happily, and to ignore the injustices and evils which require attention. The tyranny of the greatest number, even when it is not expressed in a centralized state, can be great, and their misconception of what is best can be destructive. It is possible for this view to involve floating with the tide and helping society to function in the way it sees best. This approach, therefore, involves having no anchor in biblical revelation or critique of our attitudes and economic policies. It does seem a long way from the message of the prophets or the teaching of Jesus about how often the right way is repudiated.

But there is another, perhaps less influential, tradition which goes back to Charles Kingsley, F. D. Maurice and the other Christian Socialists, to R. H. Tawney, Lord Beveridge, T. H. Marshall, Richard Titmuss and Brian Abel-Smith. The key focus of this tradition is the idea of citizenship, and the obligations and rights that accrue to citizens, because they are members one of another. Throughout this tradition the biblical norm of loving your neighbour as yourself is given expression in the opening up of what is involved in citizenship. Tawney expounds the theme of service, Titmuss the quality of public sector relationships. Often other ideas are mixed in as well, but it does seem possible that a radical realization of the politics of being a neighbour to our fellow citizens (and also to foreigners) was part of the Social Democratic idea of community.

## Radical individualism

The Liberals, by contrast, have strongly individualist roots. In the nineteenth century they distrusted any infringement of the state on the rights of individuals. This individualism was strongly attacked by the idealist political philosophy at the end of the nineteenth century. The growth of social insurance under David Lloyd George and Lord Beveridge and the development of other collective concepts meant that the Liberals modified this individualism considerably. For example, their championing of regional identity and government can by no means be called individualist. The Liberals have also worked hard on an integrated view of the business enterprise, but my perception is that, in a radically modified form, individualism remains basic to the Liberal political faith.

It has a number of components. One is the identification with people in their given situation and with their given needs which has been the hallmark of modern grass-roots Liberalism. The aim is to let people's perceptions and their agenda shape the political response rather than policies given from on high by political parties. Whether it is the disadvantaged, minority groups or local residents, it is their concerns which should be the concerns of the party. Thus David Steel began his political career by championing the cause of those who didn't feel they could cope with pregnancy. Added to this is a doctrine of rights. It is no longer individualist in the sense that the position of other people is ignored while life, liberty, property and happiness are defended. Rather, it has similarities to the theory of justice developed by John Rawls, which in turn owes more to the social contract theories of John Locke and Jean-Jacques Rousseau than to utilitarianism or natural view of rights theories. On this approach rights are negotiated with the less advantaged having the greater rights to justice.

This sounds a bit abstract, but it has direct economic implications. So, for example, an incomes policy which strongly discourages excessive pay settlements is valid, because other workers with vulnerable jobs have a right not to have costs pushed up. Thus the Liberal Democrats have an incomes policy which modifies normal market solutions. Does this not seem more Christian, allowing a direct role for issues of justice in economic affairs? Certainly, it seems more open than for example Conservative views of the economy. But I still have a problem with the underlying view of justice. Although negotiated, it remains egocentric. We have a culture which perennially squabbles about the distribution of the cake. Its values are subjective, focusing on what 'I' want, and there is no evidence that the disadvantaged have a more lofty set of values than the privileged. Biblical values and the biblical concern for loving justice go deeper than this. It is not a concern with negotiated settlements, but with what is wrong and false in our political choices, which involves a more radical process of repentance and recompense. For me this approach is too urbane to get near the political consequences of human sin.

Of course these views tend to hit the public in an amalgam of community, rights and social market philosophy.[6] A third party, however, should be developing the underlying conception of Britain's social and economic life for the next century. And here there is a curious lack of weight. Although capitalism and socialism have been repudiated, it is not always clear what is wrong in them and why it is so. Moreover, it is possible on the basis of both a social democratic and liberal philosophy to believe that there is nothing seriously wrong with popular political attitudes; they fit in with late twentieth-century humanism. Perhaps we need another set of signposts that depend more fully on biblical revelation and take us in different directions.

# Conclusion

The focus of the preceding comments has been to tease out differences of direction in social and economic policy which follow from the faith and beliefs of the three main parties, and to see whether they foreclose the possibility of a Christian direction. None of the comments suggests that Christians cannot and should not work within any of the three parties. They may suggest that the task is harder than others realize; Christians in those parties need the support of one another, and of other Christians, in a variety of ways. The deeper issue, however, is that, as we come to the end of the long period of dominance of socialist and Conservative political philosophies, none of the major parties sees our situation in a way which makes sense of the serious dilemmas we face, in Christian terms, in Britain and throughout the world.

Thus, there are dangers in using the ideological rhetoric

of secular parties, and seeing what Christian content can be shoved into it. What we need are explicit Christian political convictions, the freedom to discuss political issues in overt obedience to biblical norms, and the development of an explicit political faith which reflects, however palely, the revelation and good news of the Christian faith for politics. For me this points to the need to form a Christian Party, not a triumphalist one, but one which is explicitly committed to learning what God has to show us of the way of Shalom and justice. Christ is a leader who requires different kinds of political commitment from those which the major parties at present offer.

# The political parties and biblical principles

*Philip Giddings*

Biblical principles ● The views of the parties ●
The Conservative Party ● The Labour Party ●
The Liberal Democrats ● Conclusion

At the very beginning let me make clear where I stand. I believe that there are significant deposits of the biblical traditions in each of the main political parties so that none can claim a monopoly of the allegiance of Christians. The basic position of each party is the product of a variety of influences competing with, and complementing, one another, not least of which is the need in a liberal democracy for each party to define its position in relation to its competitors. Although I have a longstanding conviction that the position of one party is more acceptable from a Christian viewpoint than the others, this chapter is not written in support of that conviction, but rather to subject the position of each of the parties to critical analysis in the light of biblical principles.

To do this we must first clarify the relevant biblical principles. The theses which have been set out at the beginning of this volume need to be refined for analytical purposes. When applying biblical principles to contemporary parties or policies we need to be especially careful not to read back into Scripture concerns which are peculiar to our own society. True biblical principles are those which can be applied to any economic/social system, not simply to that phase of advanced capitalism which we seem to have reached. The economic/social system is subject to judgment in the light of biblical truth, not vice versa.

Similarly, while political debate in Britain has centred upon the role of the state in economic life and welfare provision, this emphasis is not immutable. It is in fact both relatively recent in Britain, and fairly unusual even amongst the advanced industrial countries of the West (where consensus on the role of the state forms the framework for other political controversies). It could indeed be argued that it is the task of Christians to change the terms of political debate rather than simply to operate within them.

Given that, I will first redefine the biblical principles in a form which makes them more generally applicable. We can then use them to determine the extent to which the philosophies and programmes of the political parties reflect biblical requirements.

# Biblical principles

The first biblical principle is *stewardship*, to be applied to human resources as well as physical ones. Stewardship means accountability, accountability to our creator God, who desires good things for his people. 'Be fruitful and increase in number' is a general mandate for mankind (Gn. 1:28). The limitations upon it subsequently revealed in Scripture are revealed in the context of a tribal, agricultural community (e.g. Lv. 25). Such limitations may be normative for other types of society, such as urban or industrial societies, but we cannot assume that they are.

The second biblical principle concerns *work*. It is

implicit in the 'cultural mandate' that mankind should find work (meaning labour) both rewarding and fulfilling. Just reward for labour is required, and wilful idleness condemned. It is not, however, immediately clear from Scripture whose responsibility it is to ensure that work is either available or rewarding, which is a crucial issue. The condemnations of idleness (2 Thes. 3; *cf.* Mt. 20) assume that rewarding work is available.

The third biblical principle is *justice* – in this context, the avoidance of exploitation of others, of ostentation, and the positive duty of sharing with those in need (Am. 6; Jas. 5:1–5). Inequalities of wealth seem to be accepted but excessive inequalities which lead to exploitation are condemned (2 Sa. 12; Lv. 19:9, 10, 13; Dt. 24:10–15, 19–22). No person should be deprived of the means of support for themselves and their family though again it is not stipulated whose responsibility it is ('Who is my neighbour?') when for some reason that does occur. The king's particular responsibility (Ps. 72) does not nullify the responsibilities of relatives, friends and neighbours.

The fourth relevant principle is political rather than economic. It might indeed be considered a derivative of the first principle, stewardship, but in this context it stands better on its own. This principle is *limited sovereignty* – the political authority (judge, king, emperor) is itself subject to divine authority, for it depends upon a divine mandate (Jn. 19:11; Rom. 13:1). That mandate is crucially limited both in its extent and in its mode of execution (Lk. 20:25; 1 Pet. 2:14). Far from being absolute, political authority can be withdrawn by God and must be contested by men when it transgresses what God requires (1 Sa. 15:22–29; 2 Sa. 12; Acts 4:19–20).

The above four principles are similar to, but less specific than, the principles enunciated in the opening theses as the basis for debate in this volume. And when we turn to the third set of theses, 17–19, we are dealing with *implications* rather than principles. As they stand, those implications are not obviously *in conflict with* Scripture, and may therefore be considered *prima facie* acceptable on biblical grounds. But for our purposes the problem with them is not their biblical basis but their political blandness. With only minor amendments, they are all 'conventional wisdom' for responsible leaders of democratic political parties. Political argument and partisan conflict is not about whether to assent to such principles, but about how to realize them, particularly when they are in competition with each other. Each thesis sets out an implicit claim upon political and economic resources. In the real world of politics it is not possible to meet all such claims simultaneously – particularly when there are other claims not mentioned here (e.g. defence, law and order) which might be held to be just as, if not more, important.

A further difficulty with these theses is that the key questions of political choice are obscured by them. Thus, for example, on thesis 13, the important issue is: what are the 'particular responsibilities' and 'legitimate rights' of individuals, institutions and the community? The political parties are in conflict not over whether the state has a task, but over what that task is in relation to the freedoms and responsibilities of individuals and institutions within the community. Similarly, on thesis 15, the issue is not whether the state has the right to tax, or the duty to make welfare provision in a dignified way. It is how to generate and distribute the resources for making such provision without over-burdening the economy, inhibiting enterprise and generating dehumanizing dependence.

In proceeding with our task of comparing the views of the parties, therefore, we shall not deal with all the theses 7–19 but rather confine the comparison to the application of the four principles set out above, which are in fact a refinement of theses 7–12.

# The views of the parties

Before we can make this comparison of the parties, however, we must establish what are their views on the role of the state and welfare provision. Unfortunately, this is an

exceedingly difficult question to answer with any degree
of precision, for two reasons. Firstly, on both the role of
the state and welfare provision, there has been, and continues to be, considerable controversy *within* the parties
as to their position (e.g., 'wet' versus 'dry' in the Tory
Party; 'revisionists' versus 'fundamentalists' in the Labour
Party). Secondly, no democratic political party will want
to risk electoral failure by being (over-)precise, and hence
(perceived to be) dogmatic, if it can possibly avoid doing
so. Qualified generalities are therefore the political order
of the day, in the interests both of party unity and electoral success. Moreover, such a strategy leaves open the
opportunity to treat each particular policy issue on its
merits when it comes to the top of the political agenda.
Study of election manifestos will not reveal precise
answers to questions about the role of the state or welfare
provision. Rather they contain either qualified
generalities about public accountability and competition,
or highly specific commitments to rates of taxation or
social benefits.

Given that difficulty, it has to be understood that any
comparison of the parties' positions can only be a *provisional* assessment, one which is itself the product of an
assessment of a party's record in government, its present
programme and the disposition of its current leadership.
It has also to be understood that political and economic
circumstances change and can result in significant
changes in the parties' position – compare, for example,
the position and programme of the Conservative Party in
1966 with 1986, or the position and programme of the
Liberal Party in 1955 with 1974.

We have, therefore, to recognize that we are dealing
with a complex and changing phenomenon. Yet we have
to note too that these institutions – political parties –
command an allegiance from their members and followers
which seems to transcend changes in party doctrine. It is
not for nothing that the members are often referred to as
'the party faithful', for the basis of their support and
commitment is something deeper than one particular set
of propositions about social and economic life. That is

something which Christians should find familiar. Commitment and faith are dispositions which religion and politics have in common.

So, with our biblical principles clarified, and our view of the parties qualified, let us examine the positions of the parties in the light of what Scripture teaches.

## The Conservative Party

The position of the Conservative Party under Mrs Thatcher was variously described as 'monetarist' or 'neo-liberal'. It is generally agreed that under her the party's position underwent a marked shift, though there is disagreement over the extent and durability of that shift. The more traditional Conservative position – at least in its post-war phase – is generally recognized to have been more collectivist. In our analysis we shall need to consider this more traditional version of the Conservative position as well as the one favoured by the current leadership.[1]

With regard to the role of the state in the economy, the present position of the Conservative Party can reasonably be described as minimalist, providing that does not prejudge the question what the minimum is. Essentially, the position is founded on the twin pillars of reaction against the growth of state power and corporatism perceived in the post-war consensus, and the positive advocacy of the virtues of enterprise, competition and individualism. There is considerable ambiguity over whether these virtues are perceived as desirable in themselves, or as the most effective way of producing the desired economic benefits – growing national (real) wealth, widely shared.

This position has produced an economic policy which has the control of inflation by the reduction of public spending as its first, and overwhelming, priority. Other priorities are the desire to reduce direct taxation to promote the personal ownership of wealth. Wealth creation is given precedence over wealth distribution. Implicit in these policies has been the acceptance of higher levels of unemployment as the price which had to be paid for the re-orientation of the economy from its previously unhealthy position. Conservative apologists will firmly assert that these policies, far from meaning the creation of higher unemployment, are the only way of reducing unemployment in the long term through a more competitive, productive economy.

With regard to welfare provision, the Conservative position has three main themes. The first is a requirement that public provision must be contained within the level of public expenditure that the economy can sustain (and here there is an important link to economic policy objectives and the reduction of public expenditure). The second is a belief that, given limited resources, provision should be concentrated upon those most in need – a preference for selective over universal provision. The third is an insistence that the role of the state should be limited in regard to provision too, so that individuals are encouraged to make their own where possible, and non-state providers (insurance, savings and similar movements, charities and the like) can make their contribution also. Those three themes rest, however, upon a fundamental recognition that the community, and therefore the state, has a responsibility to provide for the welfare of its citizens where they are themselves unable to do so.

The traditionalist critique of the current Conservative position emphasizes that the realization of the party's economic values (on which there is broad agreement) has to be subordinated to the supreme political objective of maintaining a free and united people. Thus the reduction of inflation, public spending, and direct taxation are recognized as desirable objectives – but not at the cost of a community divided by high levels of unemployment, poverty and urban deprivation. Similarly, on welfare, while it is desirable to encourage people to do more for themselves so that the state can do less, this should not be at the expense of reasonable provision for those who are in need. The difficulty with this critique is its essential pragmatism: it does not reveal where the balance between (for example) political and economic objectives is to be struck. It is hard to make a point of *principle* out of an extra half billion pounds of public expenditure on a total of around 200 billion.

When the Conservative position is characterized as 'unbridled capitalism', and the pursuit of individual material gain to the exclusion of all else, it clearly falls short of what Scripture requires. But such a characterization would be a crude misrepresentation; the reality is more complex. *Stewardship*, as we noted above, entails accountability. For more radical Conservatives this is best provided in the economic sphere by the competition of the market place. Accountability to other institutions is less effective, indeed positively harmful, as it impedes the efficient allocation of resources.

The Christian will want to insist that the entrepreneur has a wider responsibility than merely satisfying the shareholder and the market. The Christian will want to insist, too, that value cannot always be reduced to financial or market terms. There are other considerations to be taken into account, such as the health of the community, or the welfare of the workforce. In so far as it disregards those considerations, this form of Conservative ideology is in danger of making an idol of self-interest and material gain.

On the other hand, the Christian will also be aware that Scripture frequently reminds us of the essentially selfish nature of mankind; a political or economic philosophy which ignores that fact is doomed to frustration. Is the best check on individual selfishness the selfishness of others? The more radical Conservatives are clearly vulnerable to criticism at this point, whereas the more traditional Conservatives may be able to counter that criticism by pointing to restraints on market forces they are willing to endorse. In addition both kinds of Conservative can seek to counter the criticism by arguing that it is simply unrealistic to ignore market forces anyway. Attempts to control them lead either to expensive failure, or to increasing the armoury of controls to the point where individual freedom gives way to bureaucratic or totalitarian society. Scripture will support the Conservative (and others') emphasis upon responsible individualism: the practical political issue is where the balance is to be struck.

With regard to *work*, the Conservative (of either kind) will have no difficulty in accepting the biblical principle, arguing for work to be fulfilling and justly rewarded, and condemning idleness. But, as mentioned above, what is at issue is who is responsible for ensuring that work is both available and rewarding. The economic radicals argue that governments neither can nor should assume such responsibility: it is best left to the market which is the most efficient allocator of resources. More traditional Conservatives argue that governments can, and should, play a supplementary role to the market, but that their power is limited.

In the event, recent years have seen very substantial numbers of people without work – numbers which make the argument about the efficiency of the market as an allocator of resources sound rather hollow. Since 1979 the Conservative government, running counter to the post-war Keynesian consensus, has concentrated its policy efforts on improving the efficiency of the market, rather than using fiscal and monetary policies to inflate/reflate the economy so as to generate additional employment. The Conservative leadership has sought to counter criticism that its policies are heartless and uncaring by arguing that, apart from special employment measures (YOPS, TOPS, and the like) to which it has committed very substantial sums of public money, the alternatives would actually make the problem worse by rekindling inflation and thus destroying more jobs. Any jobs created by inflation/reflation would turn out to be short-term and unsustainable, a cruel deception.

Scripture undoubtedly requires that if government can, it should act to alleviate a social evil like unemployment. But before we conclude that the Conservative government falls under condemnation on that score, we must be sure that governments are able so to act (which is a political and economic judgment rather than a theological one) and that in so acting they would not create greater social evils (also partly a political and economic judgment). At this juncture the argument becomes yet more complex as the experience of other governments and other states operating other policies is taken into account.

Tested against the scriptural requirement of *justice*, the Conservative position also seems exposed, particularly in its more radical version. It appears to permit, if not actually encourage, the wealth of the few at the expense of the poverty of the many. It also appears to involve a reluctance, or refusal, to act to assist the relatively disadvantaged, such as those dependent on welfare benefits, which contrasts starkly with its willingness to act to improve the position of those who already have plenty, such as those who pay the highest rates of direct taxation. The Conservative position, on both the economy and welfare, is easily, though not necessarily accurately characterized as one of defending the interests of the privileged classes. Such a position seems to come under the condemnation Amos uttered upon the idle and exploiting rich (Am. 5, 6) and to be clean contrary to the values implicit in Jesus' teaching about loving one's neighbour, and the perils of earthly treasure (Mt. 6:19; 19:21; Lk. 10:25–37; *cf*. Dt. 15:11).

Before we accept that conclusion too readily, however, we have to consider the defence, which has four elements to it. The first is a matter of political and economic judgment. Conservatives will argue that their kind of society brings more benefits to more people than the available alternatives – that the poor and under-privileged are most effectively helped by increasing the wealth of the whole community. This is best achieved by rewarding the creators of wealth. The argument continues that more egalitarian politics not only fail to achieve their objectives, but also lead to economic stagnation – from which the less well-off suffer most. Interpreting economic history is a complex business, but the course of the British economy in the twentieth century provides as much ammunition for the Conservatives as for their critics.

The second and third elements of the Conservative defence are clarifications of scriptural teaching – that justice in Scripture is not to be confused with equality; and that it is the *abuse* of wealth which is condemned, not wealth itself, or the wealthy as such. The point about equality requires a distinction to be drawn between the

fundamental scriptural proposition that all people are
equal in the sight of God, all sinners in need of redemption (Rom. 3:23; 2 Cor. 5:10), and the radical doctrine that
all people should therefore be equal in every other respect
– wealth, position, power, status. The nearest Scripture
comes to the second proposition is the teaching that all
people should be considered or treated as equals in the
church regardless of their race, economic status or sex
(Gal. 3:28; Col. 3:11). This would seem to be significantly
different from the radical doctrine, for it says that the
differences (of race, economic status, sex) should be dis-
regarded (e.g. Phm. 16), not removed – which is not surprising, since some of the differences cannot be removed.

The point about wealth is fundamental to Conservative
perceptions. The argument is that, far from being condemned in itself, wealth is presented in Scripture as a sign
of God's favour (Dt. 8:18; 26:8–10; Pss. 25:13; 112:3). What
is condemned is the abuse of wealth, and in particular the
making of an idol out of excessive wealth. Some Conservatives would go on to argue that wealth is to be stewar-
ded by the individual (which clearly includes using it for
the relief of poverty, for example) and that this is the way
in which it is to be shared, rather than through compul-
sion imposed by the state.

The fourth element of the Conservative defence concerns what is meant by 'loving one's neighbour'. Conservatives would argue that this command applies to
individuals and is not realized when it is taken over by
the state. Indeed, they would add, the tendency is for state
aid to generate dependence in the recipient in a way
which ultimately puts his or her human dignity and political freedom at risk. This reflects the Conservative preference for individualism over collectivism.

The Conservative defence seems well made, not least
because it combines a careful exposition of Scripture with
an understanding of the realities of the human condition.
Yet one is surely still left wondering whether there can be
an adequate justification for that reluctance to use the
state's undoubted resources to relieve those who are in
want. However well defended the Conservative position

may be, it is not one which is obviously currently marked by generosity towards our needy brothers and sisters.

Our fourth scriptural principle, *limited sovereignty*, is one with which Conservatives have little difficulty in the spheres of economic policy and social welfare (though it would be different if we were considering defence, law and order or, in earlier times, religion). But, as has already been made clear, Conservatives are not impressed by the competence of the state, even (or perhaps especially) the liberal democratic state when intervening in the economy or providing welfare. The Conservative preference for individualism over collectivism is reflected in the desire to limit the power of the state and to insist upon its accountability. That, at least, is the official theory!

Overall, then, our verdict on the Conservative position must be mixed: it cannot be said to be wholly in accord with our four scriptural principles or wholly contrary to them. Which elements are to the fore at particular times will vary with the personalities leading the party, and the political context in which they are operating.

## The Labour Party

As with the Conservative Party, so with Labour, we have to be aware of differences of opinion and emphasis within the one political tradition. It is well known that the Labour Party has radical, nonconformist roots as well as Marxist ones and that the party's position at any particular time reflects the prevailing balance of opinion amongst the competing ideological strands within it. The departure of leading social democrats allowed the socialist voice to become more prominent until the mid-1980s, but the policy review pushed through under Mr Kinnock's leadership has shifted the priority back to a more social democratic position. Nevertheless, there remains a good deal of difference between, for example, the parliamentary leadership under Mr Kinnock and the so-called 'hard left' or 'Militant' factions. These differences necessarily add to the complexity of any analysis of the party's position.[2]

All sections of the Labour Party share a common belief that the political, social and economic order of modern Britain – usually characterized as 'capitalist' – needs to be changed. It needs to be changed in order that the mass of working people can share fully in its benefits. This belief combines both a rejection of privilege and disadvantage (especially when they coincide) as immoral, and an advocacy of political, economic and social equality. It implies a rejection of the capitalist principles of individualism and profit seeking, and an affirmation of collectivism and public welfare.

The Labour Party has always believed that the power of the state and the collective wealth of the community, if properly developed and fairly distributed, can be deployed to remove social disadvantage and promote equality. The substitution of the public for the private interest as the governing principle for social and economic organizations would, in Labour's view, yield a very substantial gain in public welfare. In particular, as the benefits would be shared by the many – the workers – as opposed to the few – the owners or managers – there would be an equally substantial gain in the total wealth of the community. That gain in wealth is the key to the removal of disadvantage, to the conquering of poverty, which is for Labour a supreme moral imperative.

Within the Labour movement there are differing views about the pace and timing of social improvement. The heart of the difference is this: should the conquering of poverty by improving social services, increasing welfare benefits, and redistributing wealth, await the increase in wealth necessary to fund it? Or, is the redistribution a necessary precondition to the increase in wealth which is sought? After the recovery from the Second World War, many Labour politicians saw in 'planned economic growth' an opportunity for a 'painless' redistribution of wealth. The insufficiency of economic growth for that purpose has faced the party with some hard choices as it has been constantly confronted with the question who is to pay for its programme of social improvements.

There is, however, no question that Labour is in favour

of an extensive role for the state in the economy, one much more extensive than Conservatives of either school would like. Just how extensive the state's role should be, and what form it should take, remain matters of much argument. The party's constitution in its famous fourth clause looks forward to the common ownership of the means of production, distribution and exchange. In practice, however, even the most radical of the party's programmes has not envisaged the abolition of private ownership of property. In the 1970s and 1980s the party's manifestos proposed more extensive state ownership, both in the form of direct take-overs of whole industries, and through intermediate state bodies like investment banks, but there has been much less emphasis on this since Mr Kinnock's policy review.

Much of the party's emphasis has been on extensive use of public expenditure as a means both of increasing economic activity and of relieving social and economic distress. In particular, Labour has been anxious to promote greater social equality through its economic, financial and taxation policies as well as directly through social welfare programmes. Thus the party is committed to significant expansion of government activity in housing, education, health, pensions, social security and the personal social services.

On welfare provision, the fundamental Labour position is to insist that the community must make direct provision for the welfare of its members. In direct contrast to the Conservatives, Labour preference is for universal as against selective provision, for public as opposed to private agencies, and for the priority of social objectives over financial limitations. For Labour there are two objectives: to support the disadvantaged, whatever the reason for that disadvantage; and to promote equality. Individual welfare should not, in the Labour view, depend upon the accident of birth or the unpredictable workings of the market economy.

Whilst acknowledging that the state's financial resources cannot be considered infinite, Labour is impatient of financial limitations on social welfare and is anxious to give welfare expenditure the highest priority. In preferring universal to selective provision, Labour rejects the stigmatism of the means test and the implications that benefits are privileges rather than rights. In preferring state to private agencies, Labour is not only emphasizing the importance of democratic accountability and control, but also rejecting as immoral a system which might enable some people to make a financial profit out of others' misfortune.

If we apply our four biblical principles to Labour's position, we find that on *stewardship* we have to make a judgment. Is it a well-founded assumption that state, or community, ownership, management or control of economic (and other) resources is likely to be more responsible than private, individual or corporate control? Accountability has not been the strong point of large corporations, public or private, and bureaucracy can be notoriously insensitive to individual human needs. Employees, citizens, consumers may be oppressed by large organizations or powerful institutions, whether publicly or privately controlled. Where does the balance of advantage lie? The Labour argument is that public, political, democratic control is more likely to be in the interests of the whole community than the unregulated workings of the market economy.

In assessing that argument, we have to take into account how far it is pressed. As with Conservative advocacy of the free market, so with Labour advocacy of state regulation, some would push it much further than others. Some influential Labour leaders are prepared to leave a much greater role to the market and individual choice than others, particularly since the policy review in 1989.

On *work*, the Labour Party is convinced that the state both can and should maintain full employment. Indeed, the principal motivation of Labour's current economic policy is the reduction of unemployment as rapidly as possible by direct government action. But Labour is also the party of the trade unions, and its attitudes to employment practices and industrial relations are deeply influenced by that link. Thus, the party is committed to repeal the changes in the law introduced by the Thatcher government which were designed to limit the power of trade unions and protect the rights of individual workers and employers in cases of union abuse of power, such as the closed shop. Labour advocacy of industrial democracy, or worker participation, is very much in terms of action through trade union representatives rather than, for example, direct elections from the shop floor. This seems a long way from fulfilling the cultural mandate of Genesis 1.

*Justice* is a value to which the Labour Party attaches very great importance, especially social justice. Historically, Labour has identified itself with the working class, the poor, the disadvantaged, the economically oppressed – identifications which Christians wish to make too. Labour argues that socialist values offer the best, indeed the only, way of building a just social order, by which is meant one based on social and economic equality. This is an argument which many Christians find appealing. Certainly, on the face of it, it has strong affinities with scriptural emphases like loving one's neighbour and caring for the poor, for orphans and widows, and other disadvantaged (*cf.* Jas. 1:27).

However, before we accept these apparent affinities, we must probe further into what is involved. Four points need to be considered.

The first concerns the concept of equality. Is this to be seen simply in economic terms? Does the socialist analysis lay too much emphasis on material goods? Is poverty, particularly *relative* poverty, always undesirable from a Christian standpoint?

The second point concerns method: is it legitimate to use the coercive power of the state to achieve this objective of social justice, particularly if it involves a loss of individual freedom or the creation of large and oppressive bureaucracies or groups of people who become wholly dependent on the state?

The third point concerns other values. Does the socialist analysis sacrifice other important social objectives to social justice, which may be important but not, perhaps, *that* important? Does the pursuit of equality involve a degree of social control which is in itself oppressive? Reference is often made at this stage of the argument to the experience of Eastern European countries and to Britain itself during and immediately after the Second World War.

Finally, there is the crucial question of practicability. Will it actually work? Will a socialist programme actually produce greater social justice in the sense of the poor and other disadvantaged people actually being better off (in some sense)? This is a highly controversial question of economic history, not least because many on the political right would argue that the effect of many years of neo-socialist policies has been a level of public expenditure which has produced a rate of inflation which has had disastrous consequences for the poor, who are dependent on savings or other forms of fixed income.

In assessing such arguments, Christians will want to be sure that the scriptural emphasis upon a person's relationship with God, which is the essence of his or her individuality, and the moral imperative of the parable of the good Samaritan are kept in view. It is too easy to stress individualism to the neglect of our responsibilities to our fellow men and women. It is also too easy to assume that those responsibilities can only be discharged in one particular way, whether individually or collectively.

If our third scriptural principle seems to give Labour an advantage, the fourth points to a real difficulty with the socialist position. The principle of limited sovereignty, in so far as it leads to a critique of the over-mighty state, seems to correspond closely with liberal criticisms of Labour's traditional stance. The extensive economic and social programmes which Labour advocates are seen as likely to produce a state which is too powerful, one which becomes oppressive as well as inefficient. Again, this is a correspondence which must not be too readily accepted. Scripture does not tell us what size the state should be, whether in terms of the number of officials or the proportion of GNP taken by state spending. Nor does it tell us whether the state should or should not be involved in the social and economic (as opposed to the religious) realm. Scripture enjoins on rulers an awareness of their position as subjects of a heavenly Sovereign and also a respect for the humanity of those they govern (1 Ki. 3:9; Ps. 72; Jn. 19:11; Rom. 13:1). While this rules out an absolutist or totalitarian state, it is a considerable leap of argument from there to the mixed or social market economy.

How, then, can we assess Labour's position overall? There are, I think, two crucial questions: how important is equality, in the sense of material well-being and, given the ingenuity of a fallen humanity, can any state succeed in creating an equal society without resort to unacceptable methods? Alongside those two crucial questions must, of course, go our evaluation of the social and economic conditions which Labour argues must be changed. Not to seek to change them may be seen to condone them.

## The Liberal Democrats

With the Liberal Democrats we not only have the obvious difficulty of dealing with two parties which have merged and therefore possibly two views, but also the problem that to a large extent the raison d'être of the merger, and the alliance which preceded it, was to break out of the polarization of views on the economy and social welfare which the 'old parties' have produced. The issues specified for debate in this volume may well, therefore, be considered to be the wrong issues from the point of view of the Liberal Democrats.[3]

The Liberal Democratic Party was a marriage of two traditions: the liberal tradition with its origins in the *laissez-faire* philosophy of the Benthamites, now largely discarded in the economic sphere in the pursuit of social justice; and the social democratic tradition, with its origins in the socialism of the early Labour Party.

The Liberal Democrats offer themselves as an alternative to the 'class-based parties'. They offer an approach to government and the economy based on co-operation and participation. The key to that approach is the reform of political institutions, which is seen to be the necessary condition for an effective remedy to the country's social and economy problems. A package of constitutional reforms, including proportional representation, devolution, parliamentary reform and a new Bill of Rights, is said to be a prerequisite of a new, more co-operative style for industry and commerce. Breaking the political mould of confrontation between class-based ideologies supported by industry and the trade unions would, in the Liberal Democrat view, lead to more continuity in public policy and a more co-operative and productive style for industry and commerce. To accompany constitutional reform, the Liberal Democrats advocate a major extension of profit-sharing industry and an effective form of industrial democracy.

That alternative approach is, for Liberal Democrats, a crucial background to their detailed economic and social policies which cut across the division between Conservative and Labour. They advocate selective intervention by the state. They are not hostile to private provision but advocate greater public expenditure on the social services. Alongside greater industrial democracy should go a pay and prices policy underpinned by counter-inflationary taxes on settlements above the norm.

Liberal Democrats, thus largely reject a 'dogmatic' view about the role of the state in the economy or welfare provision. They prefer a pragmatic solution to issues to emerge from the de-polarization of industry and commerce which is expected to follow from political and constitutional reform. In our analysis of this position, therefore, we have to keep in mind the wider frame of reference which it brings to the two major questions put before us.

*Stewardship* is a concept which Liberal Democrats find appealing. Accountability is a major theme of their political and economic reform proposals, and a key reason for their dislike of monopolies, whether public or private. The Liberal Party has been in the forefront of concern for the environment, again emphasizing the need for public accountability and appealing to values other than narrowly commercial ones. Within that tradition there is a strong strain of hostility to economic growth as such, and an implicit rejection in many instances of the industrial society.

The question Christians will need to ask here is accountability to whom: Where does the steward's line of responsibility lie? For the Christian the answer must be, following Genesis 1, to the creator God. There is a danger that in looking to governmental or political procedures for accountability, they become an idol. Traditionally, liberals look to the public accountability of the democratic process, as in parliamentary and local elections. Since the 1960s responsibility to the community has come to the fore instead. Precisely what this involves when applied as a general procedure in national government, in contrast to tackling some specific local grievance, is not clear. What can work successfully in the minutiae of local politics is not immediately transferable to the larger issues of the management of the national economy, the defence of the realm or running the National Health Service. In part this is answered by the Liberal emphasis on devolution and decentralization to smaller units of government which are 'closer to the people'. But that too raises a host of practical questions, especially if one desires to maintain approximately equal standards of public service provision across the whole country.

The Liberal Democratic approach to *work* has three elements: a rejection of unemployment, hence a direct attack upon it with state resources; industrial democracy and worker share ownership, on which the liberals were particularly keen; and a statutory incomes policy as a necessary condition for faster economic growth. None of this seems in direct conflict with our biblical principles, but the problems lie in whether or not it would have the predicted and desired effects.

On unemployment and increased public expenditure, the issues have been already discussed. On industrial democracy, considerable scepticism has been voiced as to whether the British workforce wishes to be represented on and participate in management in this way, and whether if it did, such a change would significantly improve workers' morale and motivation and productivity. Advocates of the policy pointed to the experience of West Germany for favourable evidence.

On a statutory incomes policy there is a similar argument. Critics point to the failure of successive attempts by past governments, both Labour and Conservative. Liberal Democrats point to the changed context their other policies would bring and to that fact that their incomes policy would be one which had been specifically endorsed by the electorate, rather than (as was the case with previous ones) a reversal of election promises.

With regard to *justice* the Liberal Democrats could again be seen to be taking a middle view, denouncing extreme inequalities of wealth – certainly a scriptural emphasis (Am. 6) – but also rejecting the deadening hand of state-imposed uniformity in the economic sphere. Again, what is distinctive about Liberal Democrats is not their view of what constitutes 'justice', but their conception of how that could be achieved – through a combination of limited state action and individualism.

*Limited sovereignty* is a concept which traditional liberals find particularly appealing, since they identify it with limiting the role of the state. In the liberal philosophical tradition – now rather a spent force within the party – this is of course a major theme. Certainly contemporary liberals are wont to deny the right of the state to intervene in many areas of social activity, a denial which is grounded in assertions about individual liberty. At this point Christians will want to proceed cautiously, especially in the moral sphere – sexual behaviour, censorship, and so on. Christians will want to affirm God's law in these areas, and in some instances argue for it to be reflected in the civil or criminal law of the land. Christians will also want to point to the distinction between liberty, a responsible expression of human self-fulfilment, and licence, an unregulated yielding to appetite (Rom. 6; Gal. 5). Christians will certainly want to ensure that assertions about human freedom take into account people's responsibility to God and the accountability of rulers to the God who gave them their mandate to govern.

It has been a common criticism of centre parties that they are strong on general principles but weak on practical policies. When assessing their position in the light of scriptural principles, we find that weakness becomes something of a strength. The general principles do not in themselves seem to be in conflict with Scripture and their outworking cannot be tested from recent evidence. It is thus on the question of practicability, and the accuracy of their diagnosis of the country's ills as political and constitutional, that most argument will be centred. This is not a question on which the Christian can claim special insights, or the Scriptures give direct guidance, apart from the reminder that no amount of political and constitutional reform will produce the ultimate answer to the human condition, sinfulness, which can only come through the grace of God by faith in Jesus Christ.

To that extent, the Liberal Democrats belong, with Labour, to that group of political traditions which takes a fundamentally optimistic view of mankind's condition in the sense that its defects can be remedied by collective human effort alone. This is a view which is not consonant with the scriptural doctrine of original sin. The difficulty for the Christian is the danger of concluding from this that mankind's social condition is so hopeless that it is not worth trying to improve it – which also conflicts with the scriptural doctrine of loving one's neighbour, and caring for those in particular need. A middle way has to be found between the belief that mankind can solve all their problems by themselves, which is unfounded and unscriptural optimism; and the belief that human attempts at social improvement are bound to fail, if not make things worse, which is unfounded and unscriptural pessimism.

# Conclusion

The analyses of these three party positions show that each can, or could claim some element of affinity with Christian principles, but none can or could claim a monopoly. Because Christian political judgments have to be an admixture of theological insight and practical wisdom, it is not in my view possible to declare that any party has an overriding claim on the allegiance of biblical Christians. Indeed, we know that godly men and women have in good conscience given their support to each of them.

It is sometimes argued in response to this that the better route for Christians would be to recognize that each of the major parties is flawed from the Christian point of view and to establish instead an explicitly Christian party. Such a party would advocate only Christian policies and would conduct its internal and external relations in a distinctively Christian way.

Such an approach is, in my view, politically naive. It is naive, first, because it is simply not possible to identify *the* Christian answer to the multitude of issues confronting a country, and especially the main ones. Christians might be able to agree on ends (though not in a way which would easily distinguish them from other parties) but could hardly agree on means – the usual point of conflict in liberal democratic societies – since judgments about means rest on economic, social and political matters in which Christians have no special insight. To say that there we agree to differ is no answer: it is not a credible posture to face an elector with, or a civil servant.

Such an approach is politically naive for a second reason. It is (sadly) simply not true that Christians do in fact conduct themselves in a distinctive fashion politically. One only has to examine the life of Christian churches (especially evangelical groups within them) to see that that argument is fatally flawed. The position would be that much worse if political tensions and disagreements were added to our differences, as they surely would in a political party whose only common interest was the religious convictions of its members.

To those political objections to the notion of a Christian party I add a theological one. Where is the scriptural warrant for involving the body of Christ corporately in politics and government? There is much scriptural encouragement to Christians to good works. There are, as we have explained above, scriptural principles relevant to the political, social and economic order. But there is, as far as I can see, no justification – never mind requirement – to organize Christians, the body of Christ, politically to apply those principles. This is surely because the practical issues involved can quite legitimately be tackled by Christians applying those principles in quite different ways.

For Christians, disagreements about politics should be neither surprising nor a cause for concern. What such disagreements should call forth is not a fruitless effort to argue them away, but a sincere determination to ensure that they can be held in fellowship and love by those who owe a common allegiance to the same Lord and Saviour, Jesus Christ.

# Response to Alan Storkey

## Philip Giddings

Developments since 1987, both in Eastern Europe and in British domestic politics, suggest that the ideological divide between state socialism and free market capitalism may be a thing of the past. Eastern Europe has abandoned not only communist forms of government but also Soviet style economic planning, replacing it with variants of the free market. Similarly, though not I think connected, the British Labour Party has reversed the more interventionist stance it had adopted in the early 1980s and explicitly recognized, in its policy review, the importance of the market. It could be concluded that in Britain the previous ideological debate between capitalism and socialism has been replaced by an argument about who can manage market capitalism more efficiently. We need also to note that the apparent triumph of democratic capitalism has been accompanied by a renewal of the debate about the moral basis of capitalism itself – though, as with socialism, there is much confusion over just what capitalism is. To some extent, therefore, the framework for political debate is shifting beneath our feet. Another example of such a shift is what has happened to the centre parties during the course of the preparation of this volume.

Alan Storkey's critique is particularly relevant to these shifts in the ideological debate. He questions the primacy of monetary values which dominate the workings of 'the market' and the related emphasis on property ownership and individual rights. He (rightly) draws attention to the importance of wider conceptions of value (worth?) which cannot be reduced to monetary terms – reminding me of the definition of an accountant as one who knows the price of everything but the value of nothing. While I see the importance of this critique, and have some sympathy with it, I do not think it is one upon which Christians, or indeed politicians, fundamentally disagree. Even Mrs Thatcher showed (over the Falklands, the miners' strike, and the Gulf conflict) that there are policy objectives which must override purely financial considerations, even when those considerations are the primary focus of government policy. Is Alan attacking the position of a straw (wo)man?

In a liberal democratic society the danger of materialism, of the worship of mammon, is ever present. But in politics it is not sufficient simply to denounce materialism, or proclaim the importance of other values or objectives, as Alan does. To be strong on denunciation and short on prescription is the classic tactic of the opposition politician but, as we all know, when the election comes, it is necessary to be more positive. Politicians, or rather governments, have to adopt and pursue practicable policies in the world as it is.

In deciding what is practicable one has to take into account the fact that financial resources are limited. Limits apply to the resources of the community as well as the state; it's not just a matter of what is raised by taxation and borrowing. That means choices have to be made. (Churches and missionary societies have to face such choices too!) Of course, the 'value' of education, health, art, or law and order cannot be expressed or compared just in terms of 'cost'. But it makes no sense either to ignore their cost, or to spend more money than is, or is likely to be, available. Somehow priorities have to be established, and limited resources allocated. To stress in that context that wealth cannot be allocated or distributed before it has been created is surely prudent, whatever the ideology, and does not entail accepting (as Alan's critique seems to imply it does) that financial considerations must always be paramount.

The real issue, it seems to me, is not whether all choices can or should be reduced to financial ones, but how financial *and other* values can be taken into account. In essence, this involves three questions: firstly, whether there is a (technically) more efficient method than a market to balance supply and demand; secondly, if one accepts that markets are the most efficient allocators of resources, whether that constitutes a moral claim; and, thirdly, if it does, whether that moral claim is an *absolute* one. In 1991 it looks as if the ideological conflict between 'market socialism' (Kinnock's Labour Party) and 'democratic capitalism' (Major's Conservative Party) seems to focus on two issues, both ones of degree: to what extent is it appropriate to supplement, or mitigate, the market mechanism; and to what extent should state, as opposed to private, non-state (including voluntary associations) means be used to compensate for market failures.

When Alan Storkey draws attention to the limitations or imperfections of market mechanisms, it is not clear to me what he is suggesting. Is he saying that there is an alternative system of resource allocation which could and should be substituted for market mechanisms in the way in which socialists used to argue for centralized economic planning? Or is he arguing that, on ethical grounds, market allocations should somehow be set aside, *e.g.* to benefit the poor, the economic under-class or some other group? If the latter, we need to know *by whom* he thinks those allocations should be set aside (he rejects the state as the mechanism on p. 162); how they would be held accountable (since they would exercise considerable power); and *how* the setting aside would be done (*i.e.* On what criteria – desert? How assessed?). The Christian will also want to know what biblical authority undergirds the answers to those questions.

Thus, my difficulty with Alan Storkey's critique is that, while he identifies some deficiencies in the Conservative, Labour and Liberal Democrat positions, he does not articulate a clear alternative. 'What we need', he writes (p. 173), 'are explicit Christian political convictions'. Yes, indeed: but precisely what? 'Shalom' and 'justice' and to 'look to Christ for leadership', are impossibly vague. Even if one could obtain agreement on the content of the first two concepts, one would still have to address the question of practicality. To me this suggests that in the world as it is there is no *Christian* political position to offer as an alternative to the ideologies of our present parties. Rather, the Christian's task is to subject those ideologies to a critique based on biblical principles, such as that attempted in my own paper. The Christian politician's task is to endeavour to pursue those Christian principles within the political tradition to which he or she subscribes.

I do, however, agree with Alan that addressing the needs of the poor and under-privileged must be a fundamental Christian concern. This is at the heart of the debate amongst Christians on the moral acceptability of capitalism. It is also at the heart of the debate about the effectiveness of state mechanisms which underlies debates about the acceptability of socialism. To pursue those themes here would be fascinating but beyond our brief. However, I would endorse one particular emphasis in Alan's critique: the importance of considering the actual outcomes of political programmes and ideologies, *i.e.* a focus on action rather than rhetoric. Defenders of democratic capitalism have to meet the challenge of the criticism that, notwithstanding their argument about wealth creation and the trickle-down effect, in practice capitalism serves to entrench the power of social privilege, and makes the rich richer and the poor poorer. Similarly, defenders of state socialism have to meet the challenge of the criticism that it too serves only to enhance the status of those who hold power and that, whatever its objectives, it not only fails to deliver a significant extension of life-chances to the mass of the people, but instead generates greater dependence. Such criticisms do need to be addressed. But pointing them out does not in itself make the case for saying there is an alternative Christian ideology of politics.

# Response to Philip Giddings

## Alan Storkey

The structure of Philip Giddings' argument is roughly as follows. There are biblical principles which can be fairly clearly stated, and implications which follow from these principles which more directly touch politics. These implications, apart from actually being rather bland, are espoused by each of the major parties in one way or another. Where they do not espouse them, they evidence practicalities and countervailing arguments which might also claim Christian and wider support. Thus each party can claim some affinity with Christian principles and none has any overriding claim for Christian support. Moreover, a party which did aim to be explicitly Christian would be naive because such a party could not establish *the* Christian answer to political issues. Further, an examination of current Christian political opinion suggests that there is no reasonable possibility of Christian agreement in this area. Finally, he sees no biblical warrant for corporate Christian political activity.

The first point of response concerns the status of principles. They have an important part to play in political life, but they depend more than is usually acknowledged on the overall philosophy and faith within which they are cast. Thus, for the liberal, justice tends to focus on individual freedom and rights. The Conservative would emphasize property rights, and the traditional definitions of justice. The radical would start from a more thorough-going concern with equality of condition. The socialist would see justice more in terms of equality of provision, and the one-nation Conservative would see it in terms of the harmony of the nation. There seems to be one principle, but actually there are as many as the underlying philosophies, and they lead to different results. Easy divorce is fine for those who major on freedom, it is a question of provision for socialists, and it would worry the Conservative. My problem with the handling of the principles is that the blandness partly comes from not locating them in the traditions which actually give the principles shape and direction. Then they can be seen, as they are espoused, more incisively.

Secondly, over against what Philip Giddings says, it is interesting that none of the major parties in any recent manifesto has explicitly espoused Christian principles. He writes, 'The Conservative defence seems well made, not least because it combines a careful exposition of Scripture'! How so? When? Where? This is wishful thinking. There was one speech in Edinburgh, perhaps in reaction to some clerical criticism, but with limited room for exposition. The links which Philip Giddings makes are made in his head, for I am sure that they are not the way in which Labour or Conservative policy is formed. There are some Christian politicians who do think this way, whose contribution is important, but limited to a small, minority input. But the normal pattern is secular principles and priorities which make no reference to Christian principles or thinking. How can this thinking stumble on such rich veins of Christian understanding? Sometimes there are echoes coming out of a Christian cultural heritage, but is it politically formative? I suggest that the Christian principles of stewardship, work and justice have been largely eclipsed by other principles, during the last ten years of government which move in another direction.

The third point concerns our expectations. The search for political answers, as some kind of infallible vision, is surely naive. There are some Christians, maybe, who still believe that from the Scriptures there is some kind of infallible deductive chain to all the answers, but that is to mistake the nature of revelation and the human response of faith. Human limitations, darkened understanding and self-justification should make us wary of any claims to provide *the* Christian answer, or any other. However, although some debate adopts that tone, usually the nature of the beast is different. People are developing a political faith; they are on the road together, and have some common guidance in their tasks. Disagreements are normal and debate is accepted, both within parties and across them. Indeed, it was John Milton who set up the rules of the game by saying, 'Let truth contend in the marketplace.' It would be very sad if Christians should retreat from this position because they are unable to handle either contending for what they believe to be true, or disagreeing with others.

Indeed, the very agenda of forming an initiative like the Movement for Christian Democracy should take into account the fact that for a century Christians have been carrying out their thinking in Conservative, socialist and liberal ideological terms, which would automatically tend to misunderstanding and a lack of shared convictions, as occurs in the wider political debate. But it is possible that as Christians discuss explicitly where their faith leads then politically, they will grow into a common understanding. It will not be uniform in policies and 'answers', but will grow from shared convictions and perceptions of politics which may be as coherent as any of the parties.

Finally, Philip Giddings finds no warrant for corporate Christian political involvement from the Scriptures. I find this view circumspect. The Old Testament is crammed full of a God-inspired, corporate political response by the nation of Israel. I do not think this was a mistake to be rectified in the New Testament. In the gospels Jesus and his disciples were treated as a corporate political body, and Jesus led his disciples in ways which had obvious political content such as eviction of the traders from the temple, entry into Jerusalem, and condemnation of Pharisees, Sadducees and Herod. Of course, Christ's message of the rule of God addressed the whole of life, and was not primarily political, yet it was also political. Because political activity in a military empire was curbed, it did not take the same form as politics today. Jesus, Peter, Stephen, Paul and a lot of other Christians, however, manifestly failed to avoid politics and corporate persecution. We should ask whether it was always by mistake that they were imprisoned or martyred. Perhaps part of our problem is the way we read corporate church organization (solely) into the word *ecclesia*, which had no such meaning. The early Christian communities were primitively organized institutional churches, educational institutions, welfare agencies, groups of families and political organizations, and were given instructions as such. It is our subsequent interpretation which has given institutional church life (only) corporate meaning, rather than the full biblical meaning of *ecclesia*. A Christian party or political movement is no less out of place in the kingdom of God than Christian marriages, churches, families or publishers. I think it is not the lack of political warrant from the Bible which is our problem; politics leaps off more or less every page. It is the fact that our culture has taught us that the Christian faith is irrelevant to the issues of justice of the day and our church theologians have taught us that theology is only about the institutional church. I believe that the biblical text annuls both these views.

# Conclusion

## Jonathan Chaplin

The foregoing discussion has concentrated on one central aspect of policy on which parties divide. Yet even with this specific focus, and with the apparatus of theses, questions and responses, it has not proved easy to identify the decisive points of disagreement. This at least serves as a reminder of the large number of different considerations that enter into a Christian judgment about which party to support, and also as a warning against easy and complacent dismissals of the party preferences of others. In view of the breadth of the foregoing discussions, this conclusion will attempt to highlight only a selection of the important issues raised. It will try to indicate where some measure of agreement has emerged on these selected issues, and to begin to clarify the outstanding disagreements. The issues selected are these:

1. What do the political parties actually stand for?
2. What is the relation between biblical principles, exemplified in the opening theses, and specific policy standpoints?

3. Do the various principles held by the political parties form a coherent whole?

4. Is there a distinctive Christian position with respect to the 'individualism versus collectivism' debate?

5. How do markets work, and what role ought the state to play in regulating them?

6. What should be the aims of social welfare policies?

*1. What do the political parties actually stand for?*

There is considerable disagreement among the contributors over what the standpoints of each of the three parties actually are. This is hardly surprising since, in view of the ideological turbulence of the 1980s, party members have been disagreeing among themselves on what their own parties stand for. And there is disagreement among contributors regarding all three parties.

The Conservative Party is publicly perceived to have experienced a fundamental, perhaps irreversible, shift of emphasis over the last fifteen years. However, while some contributors regard it as dominated now by the narrow, market-orientated, 'neo-liberal' thinking of the New Right, others imply that 'traditionalist' values are still very much alive. The claim here is that, in contrast to New Right Conservatism, such values reflect a measure of Christian influence, and that their continuing endorsement within the party enables Christians in good conscience to remain Conservatives. Some also point out that, since Conservatives remain willing to subordinate market values to higher political values such as national unity or public health, it cannot in fairness be said that market-thinking is wholly dominant.

A distinction needs to be made, however, between those non-market values which are enthusiastically endorsed by many associated with the New Right, such as strong defence, national security, and law enforcement, and those which are not, such as full employment or social welfare. Christians defending Conservatism on the grounds that non-market values remain central to party policy will need to show *which* such values are actually at work, and how effectively. Lord Griffiths (see the Appendix) in fact

208

proposes four (though these are evidently not intended to be exhaustive): community, responsibility, welfare, trusteeship. He also argues that many examples of recent Conservative legislation are clearly motivated by some of these same values. There is obviously room for debate over how far this is actually the case, and indeed over whether his interpretations of these values are adequate.

There is disagreement over the extent to which 'statism' still conditions Labour Party thinking and policy. Some contributors claim that the undeniable statist legacy within the party is still powerfully at work, though it has to be said that they have not fully documented this claim with reference to party policy since the recent policy review. Assessing a party's standpoint when in opposition is difficult, and some may feel it to be only prudent to rely on the party's latest experience in government before suspending suspicions. There certainly has been a great deal of talk about a new form of 'decentralist' or 'market-friendly' socialism. But it remains the case that current Labour policy envisages a considerably more active role for the state than the other two parties. Those who claim that this remains 'statism' need to show explicitly why their preferred policies (which, in the case of some contributors, also envisage an active state) escape that charge. Their response would be that what they wish the state to do is to 'enable' individuals and other social institutions to perform their own tasks, rather than taking these tasks over. Clearly there is much scope for fleshing out this view.

Contributors also offer contrasting interpretations of the Liberal Democrats. A central question is how far the party continues to be shaped by nineteenth-century liberal individualism, which all contributors appear to find deficient on Christian grounds. Few historians dispute that at the beginning of this century the Liberal Party's attitude to the role of the state underwent a substantial shift. This in part expressed a philosophical move away from classical liberalism to 'social liberalism'. Further, the recent influence of social democratic thought has clearly further modified the individualism of the old Liberal Party. One's evaluation of the party's present ideas and policies will thus depend in part on a Christian assessment of the adequacy of social liberalism and social democracy, both of which were partially formed by Christian thought.

Clearly, unless Christians can attain a shared interpretation of what political parties stand for, there will be little prospect of moving towards a converging Christian assessment of those standpoints. Those who regard such convergence as desirable would need to engage in a long and patient discussion on this issue alone.

*2. What is the relation between biblical principles, exemplified in the opening theses, and specific policy standpoints?*

Several contributors have felt the need to take to task not only their discussion partner(s), but also the theses themselves. This is instructive because the theses exemplify the sort of biblical and theological ideas to which Christians are appealing more and more to justify various political conclusions. It is not principally the content of these theses which attracts most criticism, but rather their character. All agree that isolated biblical texts cannot directly guide political practice (thesis 6 already rules this out), but none seem entirely happy with taking the theses as they stand as a basis for debate. The starting assumption that the overall ethical teaching of the Bible should function as a 'normative guide for Christians today' (theses 6) was not intended to be in debate but it turned out to be. The problem identified is that the theses (especially 1–13) appear to express a series of isolated biblical principles whose relationship to the biblical text and to each other is unclear (Francis Bridger and Pete Broadbent); or whose dependence on wider beliefs and values is undefined (Paul Marshall, Pete Broadbent and Alan Storkey); or whose utility in guiding political practice is in doubt (Donald Shell and Philip Giddings). Let us consider further this third objection.

Some contributors emphasize in varying degrees the indeterminacy of the theses with respect to specific policies. Statements that all politicians could endorse cannot possibly guide policy-making. Generalized statements of biblical teaching are incapable of indicating which specific policies we should pursue. Paul Marshall's response to this argument is that it is in the nature of *all* political principles, not just biblical ones, that there is what Donald Shell calls a 'looseness of fit' between principle and specific policy. Obviously no individual policies can disclose the distinctiveness of a Christian position. However, there could nevertheless emerge over time a coherent perspective which would mark out a Christian political perspective and distinguish it from, say, a Conservative or socialist one. This need not necessarily imply a call for a distinct Christian party (though Donald Shell appears to think it does), but it does imply the possibility of a political perspective which can be identified as Christian.

A key question underlying this particular debate is whether Christian political principles are commensurable with those of Conservatism, socialism or liberalism. Are they of the same kind, on the same level? Some claim that distinctively Christian political (as opposed to generalized ethical) principles, parallel to those at work in political parties and the ideologies which shape them, can indeed be formulated. Just as socialism has developed political principles like that of common ownership, or liberalism principles like equal freedom, so Christianity can (when rightly understood) generate its own distinctive political principles. Others however claim that principles which are distinctively biblical will inevitably be too general to constitute the basis of a distinctive political perspective.

It needs to be stressed here that the opening theses do not attempt to propose anything like a complete social or political theory. Theses 1–12 contain summary statements of aspects of biblical teaching pertinent to politics. These are not what is meant by the 'political principles' of common ownership or equal freedom referred to above. And theses 13–19 are simply possible general policy guidelines which might be implied from the first set of theses. A full-blown Christian political theory, like any other adequate political theory, would consist of a coherent framework of normative general concepts concerning the nature of political authority, justice, law, rights, liberty, citizenship and so on. The contributions by Francis Bridger and Paul Marshall make initial attempts at setting out some of the elements of such a theory. (Some might call this 'social theology' or 'political theology' – the labels do not matter.) Those fundamentally sceptical of this exercise, such as Donald Shell, need to demonstrate fully why they think these attempts are intrinsically unfeasible.

## 3. Do the various principles held by the political parties form a coherent whole?

The assumption of the previous section was that the political principles of a party are more or less coherent. But this after all cannot be taken for granted. Indeed many political scientists would argue that what holds a party together, and shapes its policy stance is not a coherent set of principles but rather historical traditions, the ambition for power, class ethos, changing circumstances and so on. Principles, they would argue, are decidedly secondary. Thesis 5 assumes a different view, countering the dominant post-war tendency to minimize the extent to which party policy is determined by principles, and to stress instead the external constraints of public opinion, changing circumstances and so on. It was assumed that contributors would be in broad agreement on this, but in the event they proved not to be. Although no one tackled this thesis head on, it became clear that some contributors wished to play down the extent to which principle influences policy, and preferred a 'pragmatic' approach.

Some of the disagreements can in part be accounted for by this difference. If principles play a marginal role, then there will be little point in attempting either to analyse them critically, or to mould them in order to bring Christian influence to bear on a political party. Those who hold this view are therefore more likely to stress the importance of individual Christian witness within parties, or to encourage Christians to concentrate their energies on campaigning for specific policy changes (as Fred Catherwood does) rather than constructing comprehensive alternatives rooted in distinctively Christian principles. If however party policy is indeed significantly shaped by deeply-held shared principles, then these individualist or pragmatic strategies are likely to prove ineffective in the long-term, whatever short-term successes they appear to achieve. At the risk of irritating those who feel that we are fiddling while Rome burns, we shall proceed here on the assumption that principles matter greatly.

It is one thing to hold that principles are important to parties. Some contributors go further and attempt to discover and account for the coherence among the various principles shaping party thinking. Parties do not simply hold a series of juxtaposed principles; such principles cohere within an overall ideology (or possibly two contending ideologies, which complicates the picture yet further). Each ideology ranks its principles differently, so that the meaning of any one of them is determined by its position in that ranking. A crucial conclusion is that, although parties often use the same *terms*, like justice, freedom, equality and so on, they mean fundamentally different things by them. New Right thinkers mean by 'justice' the right to individual freedom. Their definition excludes the idea of economic redistribution beyond that necessary to eliminate absolute poverty, whereas this is essential to what socialists mean by it. If these arguments are right, then it is after all not the case that, as some contributors suggest, all parties agree on the meaning of certain value-terms, differing only on their policy application. Hence the fact that all parties could endorse, for example, the opening theses of this book, should not be taken to mean that they all share the same political ends. Shared terminology conceals a substantive political divide.

It is worth exploring further the idea that a party's political principles cohere around the highest-ranking one. It may be helpful to view the principles (or 'values' or 'beliefs', as some contributors term them) to which we have been referring as arranged in a series of different levels. Consider certain specific policies of the kind which appear as manifesto pledges, such as Labour proposals to re-nationalize the electricity industry or increase pensions. This can be seen as the outworking of general policy principles characteristic of socialism, namely state ownership, and the redistribution of wealth. Going further, the principles of state ownership or wealth redistribution can themselves be seen as specifications of two broader principles, namely common ownership and economic equality. And these in turn might be seen as outworkings of an even broader socialist vision of society which Paul Marshall sums up as 'equal community', and which unifies its various principles into a distinctive ideology. If this is the case, it follows that a Christian analysis of parties will be superficial if it fails to identify such unifying or core principles.

This is a large and potentially elusive claim, and it is incumbent on those who make it to demonstrate how the mechanisms of influence between the core principle, lower-level principles, and policies actually operate. This is a complex task, but at least something can be said about it. We suggested earlier that the socialist principle of 'equal community' can be seen to support specific policies such as increases in pensions. However, as Alan Storkey points out, no 'infallible deductive chain' is involved here. 'Equal community' sums up a normative vision of social order. Several lower level principles, such as common ownership, redistribution of wealth, participatory democracy, are *compatible with* this (indeed 'comport well' with it, to use Wolterstorff's helpful phrase), though none can be infallibly *deduced from* it. And numerous particular policies are compatible with each of them, which is why socialists, just like liberals and Conservatives, disagree so often.

We have been considering the claim that there is a core political principle which unifies the various particular principles associated with socialism, Conservatism and liberalism. A further claim which deserves mention here is that these core principles are in turn determined by even higher level beliefs about the origin and nature of the world and human beings, the nature of evil, the meaning of history, the source of morality, and so on. These make up the 'underlying frameworks' (Alan Storkey) or 'worldviews' (Paul Marshall) which condition political values and principles. It is not possible, so it is claimed, to grasp the meaning of individual principles or values (at any level, presumably) apart from these broader beliefs. The implication of this line of argument is that Christians ought to ensure that their most fundamental beliefs should be allowed to determine their basic political convictions, and that these basic convictions should in turn determine the various levels of principle which eventually guide policy-making. Since there are indeed highly distinctive fundamental beliefs, it is natural to expect that the political principles and specific policies shaped by them will also be distinctive.

Again, it is incumbent on those who press this claim to demonstrate how the mechanisms of influence operate. Paul Marshall, for example, points out that differing basic beliefs about, say, human nature, have shaped the Conservative and Labour Parties, with Conservatives holding to a more pessimistic and Labour to a more optimistic view. But he does not explain how socialist optimism about human nature has influenced its political vision of equal community. A pessimistic view of human nature can indeed be used to justify socialist attempts to restrict private accumulation as much as Conservative attempts to protect it. The most recent utopians on the political scene are in fact the right-wing libertarians.

Similarly Pete Broadbent suggests that there is a correlation between the political views associated with one Christian Conservative standpoint and the 'worldview' (beliefs about God, human nature, the kingdom and so on) underlying this standpoint, just as there is in his own case. He implies that a 'kingdom ethics' tends in a leftward direction while an 'ethics of law' leans to the right. No doubt some Christians would dispute this correlation. Indeed several contributors rely heavily on Old Testament law to make points profoundly critical of Conservatism. The precise way in which 'worldview' affects specific policy questions needs more careful analysis.

4. *Is there a distinctive Christian position with respect to the 'individualism versus collectivism' debate?*

The question of how Christians should understand the proper relationship between the individual and the community recurs throughout the book. It is clear that all Christians would reject an extreme libertarian conception of the individual which strips him or her of any moral and social obligation to others, and which denies the mutuality of human beings given in the order of creation. It is also clear that all would reject a collectivism which entirely absorbs the individual within nation, state or class. None of the contributors advocates anything approaching these extremes.

However, Conservatism in particular is criticized by several contributors for its supposedly individualistic view of human relationships. The secular, self-interested individualism of some brands of Conservatism is attacked and biblical support is claimed rather for that brand of Conservatism which acknowledges that individual freedom is circumscribed by moral and social duties. Both Fred Catherwood and Brian Griffiths identify with this version of Conservatism. It is worth noting, in view of his intimate involvement with the evolution of Thatcherism, that Lord Griffiths' position cannot be classified simply as 'New Right'. Rather it is closer to the kind of American Christian 'neo-Conservatism' represented by writers such as Michael Novak.

It is also argued that biblical teaching on the divinely created corporate character of human personality rules out, from the start, a secular, contractualist individualism. Francis Bridger, for example, proposes a 'communitarian' model which reflects the diversity and complementarity of human beings and on the basis of that urges a wide dispersal of political and economic power. This view comes close to Paul Marshall's conception of a diversity of human communities each with their own task, and to what Alan Storkey refers to as the social democratic idea of community developed by Christian Socialists and others. Francis Bridger's advocacy of a dispersal of political and economic power across a variety of centres is also supported by Fred Catherwood and to a degree by Pete Broadbent. Finally, Lord Griffiths' espousal of 'mediating structures' tends in the same direction.

There may be the basis here for an emerging consensus among Christians regarding the relationship between the individual and the community. Each of the authors just mentioned would need to spell out more fully precisely which kinds of community they seek to protect, and why. Nevertheless, a degree of convergence is indeed evident around a picture of the individual as placed within a diversity of communities, each of which needs to be accorded an appropriate sphere of independence, and protected against undue domination by large organizations or governments.

A central question which this model of society evokes is of course the role of the state within it. Again there is a degree of convergence among several contributors over a view of the state as having an indispensable though carefully circumscribed function, namely to establish a public framework of just laws and policies which protects the community as a whole, and which 'enables' individuals and communities to exercise their own independent responsibilities. Several contributors stress that the authority of the state is limited by the rights of individuals and/or other social institutions. Alternatively, others warn against overestimating the capacities of individuals and institutions (like trade unions or business corporations) to regulate themselves and refrain from self-seeking actions. Underlying this difference are contrasting estimates of how deep-rooted are the structural inequalities of power and wealth in modern society, and how such inequalities are sustained. Christians disagree over the degree of power they wish the state to exercise because they disagree over where power lies within society, and especially within the economy.

217

5. *How do markets work, and what role ought the state to play in regulating them?*

The debate over the proper role of the state in the economy also depends significantly on an assessment of the legitimacy and efficiency of markets as a means of co-ordinating economic activity. None of the contributors entirely shares the New Right assumption that markets, except in a few untypical cases, are always and necessarily more efficient allocators of resources than the state or other institutions. Even Lord Griffiths, who is closest to this position, is quite clear that markets cannot be relied upon to eliminate poverty. There is little disagreement about the undesirability of turning self-interest into a virtue and erecting an economic theory upon it. Further, all contributors agree with Philip Giddings' view that markets must be subordinated at certain points to values other than the self-interested pursuit of money profitability. But there are differences of emphasis over what these other values ought to be: socialists would be more concerned with equality, Conservatives with national security, or public order.

Differences of emphasis also emerged regarding the *scope* for controlling market forces. Some are concerned about the inherent resistance of markets to government control, indeed their incompetence to engage in such control, and the resulting economic and political costs of attempting to do so. Others however place much greater emphasis on the possibility of reforming markets. The argument is that markets are, after all, not autonomous natural forces but rather human constructions reflecting variable human valuations – if we vary the valuations, we can modify the outcomes of market exchanges. And government economic policies reflect such valuations. On this view the idea of a 'free' market is mythical: governments unavoidably shape the rules which condition market outcomes, and these outcomes benefit some and harm others.

This argument is a direct challenge to a key assumption of the neo-liberal economic theory on which the Conservative leadership has been currently relying, namely that markets are value-neutral. If it is right, then the question is not primarily whether there should be *more* or *less* government intervention in markets, but *who benefits* from the intervention which must necessarily occur (and by how much). Indeed, to speak of 'intervention' in 'the market' may already prejudice the argument in favour of the neo-liberals. For on this view, the government itself is a key determinant of what 'the market' actually is. And the question of who should benefit will reflect a definite valuation.

Lord Griffiths claims that, public perceptions to the contrary, the poor as well as the rich have benefited from the way the Conservatives have administered markets over the last decade. Because he rejects the ideal of economic equality as a goal of government policy, it would present no problem to him if it could be shown that the better-off have benefited proportionately more than the worse-off. We return to the question of equality shortly. The point being made here is that even if we can agree that governments do shape market outcomes according to particular value preferences, we still have to argue about what values we should prefer.

Defenders of the market frequently warn of the risks of economic inefficiency if markets are cramped by governments, and this charge does need answering. For there is a good deal of evidence from the post-war period, not least from the UK, to support such a warning. Now Conservatives typically compare capitalist prosperity with communist inefficiency. Few deny their point, but it usually serves little more than a polemical purpose. The real contrast ought to be between different kinds of capitalism. Granted that we do not want an East European command economy, we still face a real choice between different models of a mixed economy. West Germany and the Netherlands, for example, have achieved greater relative prosperity than the UK in the post-war period, yet with more 'interventionist' government policies. And, in any case, material prosperity is not the only desirable goal. The cost of prosperity in Japan is an excessive and at times damaging sense of loyalty to one's corporation.

Thus the fact that 'wherever markets are allowed to work, the result is an increase in prosperity and jobs' (Griffiths, p. 238) may be true (though some would dispute this), but doesn't in itself prove anything. We need to ask whether, in placing ever-increasing prosperity at the forefront of government policy, we may be undermining other equally important social goals. (This question can, of course, be placed at the door of all three political parties.)

Finally, the assumption, held by defenders of the market, that markets are in some profound sense 'natural', needs critical examination. As Lord Griffiths puts it, the market 'works with the grain of human nature. ... It recognizes powerful human motives and aspirations – to own, to save, to pass on, to improve one's lot – and allows them to be channeled productively' (p. 239). Few would deny the legitimacy of this particular 'quadrilateral' of aspirations, but their relationship to other, perhaps equally powerful, aspirations – to give, to share, to belong, to co-operate, a second quadrilateral – clearly needs elaborating. One criticism levelled against Conservatism (noted but not replied to by Lord Griffiths on p. 240) is that these other human motives are actually being undermined by recent government policies. We need a conception of human nature which does full justice to both quadrilaterals, and a political philosophy which affirms each with equal enthusiasm.

## 6. *What should be the aims of social welfare policies?*
There is no disagreement over the clear biblical injunction that the state has a duty to alleviate poverty, and to provide a basic minimum standard of living to all citizens. But several criticisms are made against the way in which the Welfare State has operated in the post-war period: very high marginal rates of tax, introduced in order to redistribute wealth, have actually reduced employment, and thus indirectly contributed to poverty; service delivery has been bureaucratic and impersonal; the middle classes have benefited disproportionately from welfare benefits; no attempt has been made to liberate welfare dependents by restoring them to economic

independence. Each of these has been extensively debated for many years, and there is no space here to explore them in detail. But two points of controversy among contributors are worth considering.

The first is whether the aim of welfare policies should be to bring about greater economic *equality*. Some contributors deny that equality of condition is a Christian aim, though no one actually proposes that welfare policies ought to realize this in the strict sense. Reference is made to the Old Testament idea of inalienable family land tenure, which guaranteed everyone access to the means of production (land). Whether this was intended to secure a broadly equal distribution of land remains in dispute. Lord Griffiths, for example, interprets it to mean not that every family was allotted equal portions of land, but that each had a 'permanent minimum stake in the economy'. Moreover, whatever the precise intention of this arrangement, much complex reasoning would be needed to demonstrate its pertinence to contemporary welfare policies. Much depends on what we take to be the contemporary equivalent to land. Is it capital, property, or, perhaps, education, now a key productive resource?

A further question is whether a Christian conception of justice – a far more prominent biblical theme than equality – implies an egalitarian distribution of certain resources. If justice is defined as a pattern of distribution that conforms to the created design of society, then we might expect that the diversity of that design would call for a distribution pattern more complex than an egalitarian one. Lord Griffiths, for example, suggests that egalitarian policies inevitably centralize power and thereby undermine those 'mediating structures' which furnish the rich diversity of social life. The relationship between justice and equality clearly needs further Christian reflection.

The second point of controversy is whether the strategy of designing welfare policies as a compensation for unprincipled economic activity is fundamentally flawed. Those advancing this view believe that a better approach is to reform such economic behaviour at source by requiring companies, unions and other key economic actors to perform responsibly. The state must play a role here, but the economic actors must themselves make changes. A more responsible economy will reduce the need for a costly social policy.

As indicated earlier, no attempt has been made to comment on all the important questions raised in the foregoing contributions, nor to tackle in depth those which have been discussed. This conclusion essentially proposes a series of questions calling for further reflection and debate by Christians. If the book does no more than warn against simplistic Christian justifications of partisan standpoints it will have achieved something of value. Positively, however, it is to be hoped that the book will stimulate others to take further the continuing discussion about the shape of contemporary Christian political action. Some contributors have warned against expecting increasing convergence out of this kind of exercise, but all would wish to see Christians better equipped to engage in it.

# Appendix:
# The Conservative
# quadrilateral

*Brian Griffiths*

In an address on 'The Market' at Bristol Cathedral in 1986, the Bishop of Durham summed up Mrs Thatcher's view of society as the Conservative quadrilateral, namely: the individual – choice – the market – wealth creation. He did so to show its inadequacy as a basis for social policy and to point out its inconsistencies with Christian belief. The Bishop is not alone among churchmen in holding such views. Similar comments are being made regularly in synodical reports and statements by church leaders.

In essence, what the Bishop and others have done is to define modern Conservatism as materialistic, secular and individualistic, and that seems to be the very antithesis of the gospel. Therefore they have no option but to reject it. Meanwhile the churches have made their own position very clear: the major goal of social policy should be to reduce inequality which is something that can be achieved only through collective action imposed by government.

The Bishop's Conservative quadrilateral is said to encourage wealth creation. But even in its view of the economy, modern Conservatism is concerned with much more than the market and wealth creation, although it includes a realistic understanding of both. To understand Conservatism, the Bishop's quadrilateral needs to be complemented by a second quadrilateral, namely: community – responsibility – welfare – trusteeship. This would reflect the fact that the individual is the building brick of the community, that choice entails responsibility, that the market cannot be relied upon to provide welfare, and that wealth creation is equally if not more concerned about the future renewal of resources than their immediate use.

This is modern Conservatism as I understand it. It is not a narrow ideology based on the survival of the fittest. Neither is it a belief in unregulated *laissez faire* capitalism. Modern Conservatism is firmly rooted in nineteenth-century tradition which always sought to place wealth creation in an effective legal and institutional framework and emphasize our shared responsibility to help others who could not help themselves.

In this essay I shall argue that the Bishop of Durham's interpretation of modern Conservatism is mistaken, and that it is vital to distinguish the approach of the present government from a completely free market, *laissez faire* form of economic libertarianism, which is thoroughly secular and firmly rooted in the Enlightenment. Modern Conservatism has developed as an alternative to the post-war Keynesian, corporatist and egalitarian 'middle ground', which proved such a treacherous foundation for policy in the 1970s. If we wish to place present Conservative philosophy in a theoretical context, then it rests firmly within the Judaeo-Christian tradition. It follows that the churches should respect modern Conservatism as a legitimate political option for Christians.

# Individual and community

Judaism and Christianity have always stressed the importance of the individual. The Old Testament affirms that man is created in the image of a personal God. As Emil Brunner has stated:

> The Christian principle of the dignity of the person is unconditionally personal; the personal God creates the personal and individual human being. Thus the origin of the dignity shared equally by all mankind is not to be sought in abstract reason, nor in a general order of being, but in the will of a loving God, who addresses every man as 'Thou' and summons him to responsible being.

Hence it comes as no surprise that the commandments in the Old Testament and the Sermon on the Mount in the New Testament are both addresses to individuals. In our Lord's parable of the talents it is individuals who are endowed with talents. The gospel is an appeal to the individual. Faith is something personal. And it is as individuals that we are held accountable for our actions and called to repentance and salvation. Historically in the West, the value and dignity which people possess as individuals form the basis of human rights and the obligations of the rule of law. It would be very surprising if this left economic life untouched, not least because throughout the Bible a great deal of attention is devoted to economic life. And of course it does not. The reason for the success of the market economy is that it creates room for the individual. It rewards individuals who are enterprising, innovative and hard-working. The engine driving prosperity and employment in the last decade has been the growth of small firms and self-employment. And in almost all cases the success of small firms is associated with the leadership of one or at most a few individuals. This emphasis on the individual was also the basis for recent trade union reform in Britain.

The problem facing anyone who stresses the importance of the individual in economic life (in sharp contrast to anyone who stresses the importance of the individual in cultural affairs) is that he is immediately accused of defending greed, selfishness and individualism. *Faith in the City* stated quite categorically: 'We believe that at present too much emphasis is being given to individualism and not enough to collective obligation.' But defending the individual is very different from defending individualism. Although some versions of individualism are more attractive than others, pressed to extremes individualism is at root a deeply non-Christian, if not anti-Christian, philosophy, in which the individual is considered morally autonomous, in which contractual relationships are emphasized at the expense of natural relationships and in which the impact on personal liberty is made the sole test of legislative change.

It would be difficult for even the most committed opponent of Conservatism to argue that the policy of the present government is individualistic in this sense. Take for example three Bills which were before Parliament during 1990. *The Food Safety Bill* will better protect the consumer and raise still further safety standards and the quality of food produced and sold in Britain. *The Environment Protection Bill* will improve pollution control, reform the system for dealing with waste disposal, strengthen the law on litter and intensify protection of the countryside. *The Broadcasting Bill* will deregulate commercial television while at the same time preserving quality for Channel 3 in a number of different ways; it will also retain the existing remit for Channel 4 and place the Broadcasting Standards Council on a statutory basis. This is not *laissez faire*! Each of these Bills strikes a balance between encouraging a thriving market, protecting consumers and setting standards. As with so many other examples which could be given, it is quite wrong to suggest that the major, if not the only, test made by the government in framing new legislation is whether it reduces state intervention.

Individualism also strikes at the heart of the Christian view of society. If the Old and New Testaments affirm one thing, it is that we are not isolated individuals bound together simply by contractual relationships. Israel in the Old Testament was a community. Each of the twelve tribes was a community. And the essential core of each community was the family, which is the archetype of all communities. Many of the pentateuchal laws, such as those relating to the Jubilee and usury, had as their objective the preservation of the community.

The New Testament also emphasizes the importance of communal life – whether through the example set by our Lord and the disciples, or through use of metaphors to describe the church, such as the household of faith, the vine, or the building of God. Most powerful of all metaphors is the body of Christ. Our Lord in the New Testament sums up the laws of the Old Testament as just two precepts: love of God and love of neighbour. Therefore Cain's question 'Am I my brother's keeper?' is answered directly by our Lord's words: 'Love your neighbour as yourself.'

What, however, modern Conservatism refuses to do is equate this necessary concern for others with the pursuit of equality or corporatism. All too often in the eyes of the church in recent years the litmus test of compassion has been whether egalitarian policies are being advanced. The presumption is that equality, corporatism and growing state provision are the only authentic expressions of Christian concern in society. Anything else is dismissed as individualism or materialism. To quote one prominent democratic socialist: 'We can only fulfil our obligations to our neighbours when society takes collective decisions about individual rights and individual responsibilities.'

# Equality and justice

It is worth considering why the churches have come to equate social concern not just with equality of opportunity or equality before the law, both of which are vital to a creative society, but also with equality of result or equality of outcome.

'A liberative gospel must echo the egalitarian torrent which we find in the New Testament.' Those holding this view expressed in the 1989 report *Living Faith in the City* believe that equality is a Christian virtue and argue that metaphors such as the body of Christ, while originally used as a description of the church, should not be limited to it. They should become the vision for human society as a whole. If the state is concerned to legislate for the common good, this will mean implementing policies to reduce inequality and to extend state provision of services. Three pieces of evidence are usually advanced to support this idea that equality is a Christian ideal: the fact that all persons are created equal in the sight of God; the various laws in the Pentateuch describing the political economy of Israel (such as those relating to the restoration of land at the Jubilee, the cancellation of debts every Sabbath year or the prohibition of usury) which involve a redistribution of income and wealth, or attempt to prevent inequality developing; and the so-called 'communism' of the early church.

Using such precedents to justify egalitarian policies gives rise to a great many difficulties. The fact that all people are created equal in the sight of God is an important basis for equal human rights and equality before the law, but this is hardly sufficient in itself to require, for example, after-tax equality of income with all the distinctive effects that must follow on. Similarly, in no sense can the laws of the Pentateuch be said to have had *equality* as their purpose. In fact, they neither sought nor achieved equality. Their objective was to ensure that each family retained a permanent minimum stake in the economy, and that economic life did not undermine the cohesion and stability of Israel as a nation. Then again, the sharing of property which characterized the church at Jerusalem in the early years was entirely voluntary, and cannot be a proper model for state concern. Christians were to meet the needs of the poor within the growing Christian church through their own personal charity. Such giving was always voluntary, and the basis of St Paul's argument when the church at Jerusalem was in distress was an appeal based on compassion and fairness.

Theologians over the centuries have rarely interpreted the practice of the early church to mean that governments should legislate for economic equality. With the exception of certain sects and cults, the social concern of Christians has always been social *justice*, conceived as fairness but not equality. In any case, one crucial point which is so often overlooked by those who relate Christianity to

equality is the unbridgeable gulf between the two communities of the New Testament – the church and the world.
No one can read the New Testament without a profound
sense that although the church is in the world, it is a wholly
different community. It was this understanding, and his
own personal experience in opposing apartheid, which led
the former Archbishop of Cape Town, William Burnett, to
say:

> The fact is that to attempt to superimpose a
> particular spirituality, a teaching on Christian
> ethics, or social action, as an expression of the
> love of God upon lives that do not know his love
> for them in Jesus Christ, and who do not experi-
> ence the power of his Holy Spirit, is an exercise
> in futility. It leads to frustration, boredom, irrit-
> ation and unbelief. To renew society with
> unrenewed Christians is like a non-swimmer
> trying to rescue a drowning man.

It is therefore quite invalid to move from the practice of
personal generosity based on a voluntary appeal within the
early Christian churches to the pursuit of equality in a
pluralistic and secular society using the coercive power of
the state.

## 'Little platoons'

Christian theology reminds us of our obligations to our
neighbours, but it offers no justification for compelling
others to submit to the pursuit of economic equality by
governments.

Participation in the life of modern democracies is not
confined to government action or even to the political
process. People participate in the life of a community by
belonging to or participating in a variety of institutions –
family, parish, school, neighbourhood, church, work
place, trade unions, charities, professional bodies and so
on. They do so because it is only by joining with others that

they feel fulfilled as individuals. In this sense the conflict between the individual and the community is more imaginary than real. As Charles Murray has observed, 'The pursuit of individual happiness cannot be an atomistic process: it will naturally and always occur in the context of communities.'

In 1790 Edmund Burke described these communities as 'the little platoons' of our society. More recently they have been referred to as 'mediating structures', namely, those institutions which stand between the individual in his private life and the large institutions of public life, especially the state. It is the absence of such unofficial agencies that helps to explain the horrors of totalitarian states.

These little platoons are important for a number of reasons. They enable us, as Burke so clearly argued, to develop a sense of community:

> To be attached to the subdivision, to love the little platoon we belong to in society, is the first principle (the germ as it were) of public affections. It is the first link in the series by which we proceed towards a love of our country and to mankind.

These little platoons are the cradles of civic responsibility. They provide diverse ways in which individuals are relieved of their isolation. By joining together for limited purposes, but always to do with the common good, people are able to transfer the values of individual life to the larger institutions of society. Hence they are able to identify themselves much more with the greater community.

The little platoons are also a way of empowering people. They help people 'make a difference' by improving the communities in which they live. The churches are not alone in pointing to the feeling of powerlessness which exists today in the face of large bureaucratic institutions in modern society. Recently a journalist friend (who is most definitely not a Conservative) observed how a recent visit to Liverpool taught him that the options facing local residents in the inner city allowed them little choice because they were all in the public sector: council housing, local education authority schools, public transport, welfare benefits, public sector employment. It is this politicization and centralization that explains why the mediating structures that thrived in the nineteenth century have become so weak. Policies which attempt to strengthen these structures hold the key to any lasting regeneration of our inner cities.

Despite the aggrandizement of government the little platoons remain significant providers of welfare. The family which is the archetypal community is also the primary supplier of education, health care, training and other welfare, in addition to food, shelter, moral support and love. Indeed, most of the welfare enjoyed by our society is provided through families. Apart from the family, the many charities and organizations of the voluntary sector are also generous and pioneering providers of welfare. In addition there are schools, community organizations and the welfare provisions of companies and trade unions.

Finally, mediating structures are important as the sources which generate and maintain values in society. The family, the school and the churches are particularly influential sources of values. When such institutions are suppressed, the state itself becomes the major source of values, almost invariably with disastrous consequences. Totalitarian governments hate mediating structures because they challenge their attempts to exert total control over society. Meanwhile modern democracies require robust independent mediating structures for their health and survival.

These four functions of mediating structures – the development of civic virtues, the empowering of people, the provision of welfare and the generation and maintenance of values – make them of vital significance to a modern democratic society such as ours. That is why Conservatism attempts to strengthen them.

For schools which do not have voluntary status, large local education authorities can seem bureaucratic, impersonal and arbitrary, as can housing estates for tenants, and the NHS for patients. Schools will be strengthened as communities by effective arrangements for parents and independent persons to be appointed as governors, and for them to have greater financial powers, the right to appoint staff and the responsibility to oversee delivery of the curriculum. By enabling tenants who do not wish to buy their council houses to opt out of local authority control through the Tenants' Choice Scheme, the government is empowering them, and creating the opportunity for power to be exercised at the level of an individual estate rather than at that of the town hall. By allowing hospitals to have trust status, rather than just being one of the many 'units' in the regional health authority, the government is creating conditions in which the local community spirit can flourish. In all cases where the government has restored former freedoms there is also a transfer of power from local authorities or from the National Health Service; but it is a downwards transfer to a more basic level – the individual school, the individual housing estate, the individual hospital – not an upwards transfer to central government.

It is important to notice two particular implications of mediating structures. First, their growth and their robustness would be severely limited if government attempted to pursue a policy of economic equality. The pursuit of equality can be achieved only by the centralization of power which must be hostile to the development of the 'little platoons'. Smaller communities are bound to emphasize local differences, easily denounced as 'inequalities' because they produce variety and hold out as centres of excellence against central controls. A state determined to achieve equality of outcome would have to suppress the 'little platoons'. In this context, nothing has been more distorted than Mrs Thatcher's remark during an interview: 'There is no such thing as society.' It is worth placing it in context:

> I think we've been through a period where too
> many people have been given to understand that

> if they have a problem it's the government's job
> to cope with it. 'I have a problem; I'll get a grant.'
> 'I'm homeless; the government must house me.'
> They're casting their problem on society. And,
> you know, there is no such thing as society.
> There are individual men and women, and there
> are families. And no government can do any-
> thing except through people and people must
> look to themselves first. It's our duty to look after
> ourselves and then, also, to look after our neigh-
> bour. People have got the entitlements too much
> in mind, without the obligations. There's no
> such thing as entitlement, unless someone has
> first met an obligation.

What this passage plainly says is that society does not exist
as an abstraction set apart from the people who compose it.
Society is us, immanent rather than transcendent. Mrs
Thatcher's words were an affirmation of the importance of
personal responsibility and of the need for people to face
up to the consequence of their own actions. They were in
no sense a denial of the importance of the community or of
the value of all those mediating structures which are
crucial to the well-being of society.

# Choice and responsibility

Archbishop William Temple in his book *Christianity and
Social Order*, published in 1942, set out to develop what he
called Christian social principles. His fundamental principles relate to God and man, but in introducing the three
principles which are derivative of these – freedom, fellowship and service – he had this to say:

> The primary principle of Christian ethics and
> Christian politics must be respect for every per-
> son simply as a person. If each man and woman
> is a child of God, whom God loves and for whom
> Christ died, then there is in each a worth

> absolutely independent of all usefulness to society. The person is primary, not the society; the State exists for the citizen, not the citizen for the State. The first aim of social progress must be to give the fullest possible scope for the exercise of all powers and qualities which are distinctly personal; and of these the most fundamental is deliberate choice.

On the basis of this remarkable statement, Archbishop Temple went on to argue that:

> society must be arranged to give every citizen the maximum opportunity for making deliberate choices and the best possible training for the use of that opportunity. In other words, one of our first considerations will be the widest possible extension of personal responsibility; it is the responsible exercise of deliberate choice which most fully expresses personality and best deserves the great name of freedom.

Since 1979, extending choice has formed a central aim of government policy. In most areas it has been an outstanding success, in the teeth of fierce opposition. So far, about 1.4 million council houses and flats have been sold by local authorities in Great Britain – roughly 20% of the total stock of eleven years earlier. Large numbers of employees have bought shares in privatized state companies. Trade union members have been granted choice over the election of officials and decisions about strikes. Parents' rights to choose schools for their children in other education authorities have been enshrined in law. More than seventy schools have so far sought or are seeking to opt out of local authority control. To judge by the demand for places, parents and teachers keenly value the choice afforded by the newly created grant-maintained schools and city technology colleges. Some eighty major hospitals have sought independent trust status as part of the health service reforms. The full impact of this extension of choice has not yet been felt in society, but it will emerge during the 1990s as it becomes embedded in the ordinary course of affairs.

Whether in private or public sectors, choice is an important counterbalance to the entrenched power of producer interests. Choice forces producers to be more responsive to the short-term needs of those they serve. Consumers, parents, patients and tenants will all receive a better quality of service as the range of choices with which they are provided is widened. Choice encourages innovation and variety, although choice will be more restricted in the public than in the private sector.

One objection to extending freedom in this way is that the increased choice of some is seen as a restriction of choice for others. What if extending parental choice leads to certain schools being identified as inadequate and so liable to cruel rejection? What if council house sales reduce affordable housing for others? It is important to notice that when choice is extended in the public sector, certain checks and balances have been built in to prevent those kinds of unsatisfactory outcome. Take, for example, the case of education. Parents will choose those schools they think best for their children. The result is that governors and the local education authority will no longer be able to do nothing about the schools which have serious problems that need to be addressed. Under the previous system in which choice was limited, the weaknesses of poor schools were not exposed, and so parents would have no choice but to put up with inadequately-run schools. Increasing choice certainly means that good schools are in immediate demand, but it also means that problem schools will be highlighted, so exerting pressure on governing bodies and local education authorities to make improvements and hence raise standards throughout the authority. In a world of choice this becomes a major function of the LEA.

It is important to recognize that the case for extending choice is not just concerned with efficiency and money. Council houses have been sold not with an eye on the revenue which sales raise, but so that families can gain independence and provide for their children. Share ownership has been extended not just to strengthen accountability but to give as many people as possible a direct share in wealth creation. Choice in education has been widened not just so that schools can be run more efficiently but as a way to raise standards of achievement – in examinations, sport, arts and at a personal and moral level. Trade union reforms have been implemented not just to improve productivity through more flexible work practices, but to prevent the intimidation of individual trade union members. In other words, extending freedom of choice is not simply freedom from certain types of state provision and control, but freedom for schools, hospitals and housing trusts better to satisfy the individual aspirations of those they serve.

Archbishop Temple also recognized that extending choice cannot be divorced from extended responsibility. The extension of personal choice is at the same time an extension of personal responsibility. Choice for parents implies more direct responsibility for their children's progress. Freedom for head teachers means more direct accountability for the way they run their schools. Alongside the right to buy goes the responsibility of ownership. A more independent status for hospitals means greater accountability for the service they provide to patients.

Extending choice and responsibility changes the ethos of a society. It encourages greater private and voluntary initiatives elsewhere in the community. The 1980s saw the business community in the UK accept major new social responsibilities over and above their contributions to charity. The first enterprise agency was started in 1978. Today there are over 300 local enterprise agencies which provide a comprehensive national advisory service for small businesses.

Business leaders have come to recognize that their enterprise, energy and skills must be put to wider use if urban regeneration is to be more than charity. The quality of local leadership is crucial to creating confidence both within the community and with investors. This confidence will affect investment and development. For example, Business in the Community has grown rapidly over the past decade and, in collaboration with the CBI and the

Phoenix Initiative, business leadership teams are now established in more than twelve cities, bringing together senior business leaders and representatives of government, trade unions, education and the voluntary sector, to help in economic regeneration, the development of enterprise, partnerships and compacts between business and schools, community projects and training. When parents and business people were given the opportunity to be school governors, there was widespread scepticism whether sufficient numbers could ever be found. The response has been outstanding, as has the readiness of business leaders to direct the new Training Enterprise Councils.

Such initiatives to strengthen community neighbourliness and responsibility have not been confined to business. Neighbourhood Watch schemes were started in 1982. Now there are over 80,000 covering three-and-a-half million homes. They are now also being extended to other Watches covering pubs, schools, hospitals, farms and industrial buildings. In total, these Watches are growing at the rate of roughly 400 a week. Also in the field of crime there are now more than 350 Victim Support schemes which cover most of England and Wales – another rapidly expanding movement.

# Markets and welfare

The third element of the Bishop's quadrilateral is 'the market'. In discussing this the Bishop raises the question 'How much faith should we have in the market?' and answers with complete certainty, 'None whatever.' To him 'there is no such thing as the market' because it is a theoretical abstraction and even if it did exist it would not be a proper object of faith. The market should be something we can handle, not something which controls us.

In this answer 'the market' is being used in three separate senses. If the market stood for a political philosophy of unchecked individualism and libertarianism, in which the only criterion for change was removal of restrictions by government, then the Bishop would be right to answer that we should put no faith in such a system. But by his own response, he seems to use the market in a second sense, namely as a shorthand for the analytical tools of economics. Like any scientific discipline, economics involves abstraction from the real world. But such a method should not be judged invalid simply because it involves abstraction: its usefulness depends on how well it can explain actual phenomena such as shortages and rationing, price changes and unemployment. Economics is subject to severe limitations but remains a powerful tool of analysis.

Where, however, the Bishop's certainties are most misleading is in using 'the market' to refer to an economic system characterized by widespread property rights, and free enterprise tempered by quite extensive government intervention in economic life and then claiming that we should have no faith whatever in this kind of arrangement.

Wherever markets are allowed to work, the result is an increase in prosperity and jobs. The remarkable contrast in economic performance between Asia-on-the-Pacific and Latin America over recent decades can be traced to the superior wisdom of faith in the market over faith in the state. Most dramatic is the contrast between East and West Europe in the period after the Second World War. The prosperity of Western Europe is due to innovation, high productivity and high investment as the result of private enterprise. In Eastern Europe the comprehensive reliance on state planning to direct economic life has been nothing short of a catastrophe, with the results being most tragic where the beliefs are strongest and the controls most comprehensive. In the USSR the shops are empty, the morale of workers low, enterprise has virtually disappeared and innovation has to be imported.

In the midst of its difficulties one source of inspiration for Eastern Europe has been the present Conservative government. They remember that in the 1970s the British economy was characterized by high inflation, rapid growth of the public sector, marginal rates of income tax of 98%, extension of state ownership of industry, increased legal privileges for trade unions and arbitrary wage and price controls. And they also remember that the result was the

'British disease', namely low productivity, inefficiency and growing unemployment. Against this worsening background, the turnaround in the last decade has been dramatic – the growing juggernaut of government halted, enterprise encouraged, taxes cut and controls lifted. And they also know that the result has been a growth in the national income of approximately 25%, the creation of nearly 3 million new jobs and a fall in unemployment of nearly 1½ million. The East Europeans' interest in privatization, the growth of small businesses and retraining schemes are because they aspire to turning round their own economies in the same way.

The success of the market economy in creating wealth and jobs should not come as a surprise. The market derives its strength from the instincts and abilities of ordinary people. It works with the grain of human nature and provides a variety of ways through which the imagination, energy and talents of people can be fulfilled. It recognizes powerful human motives and aspirations – to own, to save, to pass on, to improve one's lot – and allows them to be channelled productively.

We can also explain the success of the market economy in a theological context. All the essential elements which make for the success of the market economy can be found in traditional Jewish and Christian teaching – the physical world as God's world, the mandate to subdue and harness the earth, the significance of work in a context of vocation and calling, the need for private property rights and the rule of law, a recognition by the state of the creative and innovative character of people, and the importance of a government's role in enforcing justice.

Similarly, the ultimate reason for the failure of socialist economies lies beyond economics. At one level this failure can be explained by widespread state ownership, control and planning. But what is critical is the philosophy out of which these have grown: a materialism which leaves no room for any spiritual dimension in the world of work, a failure to respect the dignity and therefore the freedom of the individual, and a 'fatal conceit', to quote Hayek, in the power of human knowledge and therefore in our ability to plan and control. Socialism is flawed by its view that the spiritual dimension is irrelevant to the material, the grudging concessions made to private property and the lack of opportunities which it gives for individuals to fulfil and express themselves.

# The market and 'the poor'

One criticism of the market economy often made by spokesmen of the churches is that the wealth it creates does not 'trickle down' to the poor. The energetic, the talented and the fortunate do well, but there are large sections of people, we are told, who are excluded from the fruits of wealth creation.

Three kinds of evidence are typically used to argue that 'the poor' lost out under Mrs Thatcher's Administration: the growth in the number of those on low incomes, the widening of income differentials between high and low income categories, and the alleged fall in the real value of benefit in the 1980s compared with the 1970s. In 'How Well Have Britain's Poor Fared?'[1] Frank Field goes further than this. He talks about 'the poor' having been expelled from full citizenship and excluded from rising income during these years by the four horsemen of the apocalypse, the most powerful having been unemployment. The result has been a growing underclass who live under a form of political, social and economic 'apartheid'.

A number of comments need to be made about this.

Firstly, insufficient credit is given to the power of the market economy in creating jobs. If growing unemployment was a major factor in increasing 'poverty' in the early 1980s, the subsequent fall in unemployment must be a major factor in reducing 'poverty'. We have had eight years of sustained growth in Britain at an annual average rate of over 3%, and the creation of more than 2¾ million new jobs since 1983. Unemployment has fallen since July 1986 by 1¼ million in total, and in all regions of the country.

At the same time, part-time work has flourished. Over 6 million people are now employed on a part-time basis, and less than 8% of these say it is because they could not find a full-time job. Such increased flexibility of working clearly suits the needs of those who prefer to work on a part-time basis. A growing economy provides opportunities for people of all income levels, including low ones, to improve their position and directly reduces those categorized as 'poor'. Wealth creation is by far the most enduring method of job creation – far more powerful in the longer term than job creation programmes.

Secondly, the real growth in the 80s would not have occurred if the thrust of government policy had been egalitarian. During the 1980s there was a dramatic increase in the purchasing power of income even though relative incomes widened. For example, between 1974 and 1979 a person on average earnings had, after tax and inflation, an increase in real take-home pay of 0.6%. By contrast, a person on half-average earnings had an increase in real take-home pay of 4.2%. Real income increased slowly but inequality was marginally reduced. Since 1979 a person on average earnings has had an increase in real take-home pay of 33.8% and on half-average earnings an increase of 26.8%. In recent years there has been a large increase in people's absolute levels of real income, but a widening of differentials between high and low income levels.

Thirdly, figures from the Department of Social Security show that, before housing costs, all groups in the income distribution experienced improvements in real income between 1981 and 1987; the median income of the lowest 10% rose by nearly 10%. Even between 1979 and 1987, that is including the period of the 1979–81 recession, each group saw its income improve before housing costs. Median incomes rose, too, for all groups between 1981 and 1987 after housing costs, although measuring income in this way takes no account of the choices people make about housing, and the substantial growth in owner occupation. (In 1987 people in mortgaged households comprised nearly a third of the lowest decile after housing costs.) This encouraging picture is not diminished by the assertion, based on references to basic rates and single components of social security benefits, that the poor became worse off during the 1980s. The Department of Social Security's data, which takes account of disposable income from all available sources, shows that between 1981 and 1987 the real incomes of those in receipt of income-related benefits in the lowest 10% of the income distribution rose by between 4 and 8%, depending on the measure used. Nor are the improvements measured before housing costs solely attributable to higher Housing Benefit consequent upon increased rents. In fact, increases in Housing Benefit account for only a very small fraction of the overall rise observed for the lowest decile before housing costs. Certainly the statistics do not present a single, unambiguous picture. They rarely do. But taken as a whole, the evidence hardly allows the argument that increased wealth resulting from sustained economic growth in the 1980s has done nothing to help the least well-off. On the contrary, all the indications are that 'trickle-down' had a significant and continuing effect throughout the decade.

Fourthly, social policy is not helped by grouping millions of people together and labelling them as 'the poor', the 'expelled' or 'the underclass'. The problems facing the frail elderly, the long-term unemployed and one-parent families are all very different and call for very different responses. *Faith in the City* rightly pointed to certain inner city areas and outer housing estates where unemployment has remained very high; few tenants have bought their council houses; truancy in schools is high; teenagers are exposed to a drugs culture; and the proportion of one-parent families is well above average. In these situations families are more than usually dependent on the state. Therefore it is in these areas in particular that the government's education and housing reforms and inner cities policies offer the greatest hope. Policy has not been premised on some vague faith in the market solving all the problems of those on low incomes. The government has sought to strengthen the market economy; but at the same time it has also sought to ensure that people from all backgrounds are able to benefit. Hence these particular reforms.

The initial task is to encourage wealth creation: to

develop enterprise through establishing small workshops linked to training programmes. Children can be helped by directly improved standards through the national curriculum, and overall standards raised by greater parental choice, different kinds of schools and increased contact between the business community and the schools. At the same time estates can be improved, homes provided with gardens and improved security, through a diversity of ownership and the use of Tenants' Choice. All of these changes will give an increasing number of people a direct and meaningful stake in their communities. Getting this to happen is hard work but it is something to which the government is totally committed and there is no doubt that it is working. The full fruit will emerge in years to come.

# Wealth and trusteeship

Since 1979 creating the conditions in which wealth creation can flourish has been a vital objective of government policy.

This stems from a belief that every person should find it rewarding to be able, in Adam Smith's words, 'to better his condition' if he chooses to do so. By extending home ownership, share ownership and occupational pension schemes, families are becoming more financially secure and less dependent on the state, and hence in a better position to cope with the contingencies of life as well as to reach out to help others. Increasing wealth also means increasing resources for government: the more rapid the growth of income the greater the resources government receives and hence the greater the resources available for improving education, welfare, the Health Service and affordable housing. And then, as we have just seen, wealth creation is a crucial source of job creation.

One point which should not be underestimated is the effect which the successful regeneration of the corporate sector has had on its ability to play a wider role. As we saw earlier, the 1980s saw the company sector in the UK assume a wholly new role in the community. Were it not for their commercial success this would never have been possible.

One objection frequently raised against the creation of wealth is that it encourages a materialistic philosophy of life. Usually this is made as an obvious assertion – the 'loadsamoney' society and the 'yuppie' culture. The reasons for linking wealth creation with materialism are seldom specified but would probably include the claims that: wealth creation satisfies personal needs but has little regard for the wider community; the methods used may be questionable as people see the possibilities of cutting corners; the competitive pressures on those working in successful companies tend to create an imbalance between work and everything else. Some would also probably argue that increasing prosperity is almost by definition an increase in materialism – possibly using as evidence John Wesley's great sermon on 'The Use of Money' which, while advocating 'gain all you can', 'save all you can' and 'give all you can', also observed: 'the Methodists grow more and more self-indulgent because they grow rich'.

The Bible has a good deal to say about wealth and materialism. Indeed, both figure quite prominently in the teachings of the Old and New Testament. The task of wealth creation is a description in contemporary language of God's command to man to 'subdue the earth' and to rule over it. The Hebrew words for 'subdue' (*rabash*) and 'rule' (*radah*) are particularly strong: the former literally means to stamp on or bring into subjection while the latter is frequently expressed as dominion. Man is given the responsibility to harness the resources of the physical world. Although originally applied in the context of agriculture, this command easily extends to extraction, manufacturing and services. The implication is not simply that wealth creation is a legitimate activity. The command surely implies that the task of wealth creation is fundamental to our trusteeship of the world and that in responding to it we also discover how work is basic to human fulfilment. Far from having a sense of guilt, therefore, about advocating wealth creation we should acknowledge that it is basic to our understanding of the creation order.

But the command to subdue and rule is not the freedom to destroy and waste. Our enthusiasm for wealth creation must be balanced by an equal enthusiasm for environmental protection. Man is a trustee for God's world. Although there may be extensive debate over the causes and effects of the risks to our planet and the precise policy choices which have to be made, there can be no doubt about the moral basis from which we start and in which the debate must take place.

It is above all clear that wealth creation can be sharply distinguished from materialsm. According to St Paul it is the love of money which is the root of all evil because 'they that will be rich fall into temptation and a snare and into many foolish and hurtful lusts'. Jesus's censure of wealth is addressed to the rich: 'Woe to you that are rich ...'; 'How hard it is for those who have riches to enter into the Kingdom of God'; and to the rich young man, 'Sell all you have ...' Jesus and his disciples were probably neither very rich nor very poor and would today be categorized as self-employed tradesmen or craftsmen, or small businessmen. Jesus warns against 'covetousness' but this is quite distinct from the normal world of work and it is wrong to interpret warnings addressed to the very rich as a blanket condemnation of the whole process of wealth creation.

Although wealth creation cannot be labelled materialism, when Jesus does speak on economic issues he introduces a distinctive standard of values: 'Be not anxious about the morrow ...'; 'Seek ye first the Kingdom of God and his righteousness ...'; 'You cannot serve God and Mammon ...' It is hard not to miss the meaning of injunctions such as these but infinitely more difficult to keep them. As Dean Inge remarked, 'Christ sits very lightly to all this paraphernalia of life'; and after making the case for social concern he concluded the argument with a statement which almost seems foreign to the church today:

> However long may be our lease of our present home; however splendid may be the possibilities which applied science seems to promise us,

245

this earth is but the shadow of heaven, an imperfect copy of the eternal and spiritual world which surrounds us and penetrates us, closer than breathing and nearer than hands and feet, but invisible and impalpable. There, in the eternal world, is the home of the ultimate values – Goodness, Truth, and Beauty – which give to our visible world all of worth that it possesses; there is our heart's true home; there is the presence of God. Against this spiritual world, as a background, is set all that we admire and love here on earth. And so, with all our enthusiasm for making life a better and happier thing for our brethren, we must never forget the words of St Paul: 'We look not at the things that are seen, but at the things that are not seen. For the things that are seen are temporal; the things that are not seen are eternal.'

## Values in society

In this essay I have sought to show that the Bishop of Durham's Conservative quadrilateral is a caricature of modern Conservatism. Any serious discussion of wealth creation must confront the need for individual choice and the freedom of markets. But modern Conservatism cannot be understood within the narrow confines of economics, let alone economic libertarianism. Alongside its advocacy of the market it is concerned to defend those values which are at the heart of a responsible society – on the one hand a sense of personal duty and self-reliance and on the other a personal obligation to those in need, to future generations and to our environment. At the same time the Conservative vision of society is not just an atomized collection of relentlessly self-seeking individuals pursuing their narrow self-interests. It seeks increasingly diverse and strengthened communities in which individuals feel at home and through which they can fulfil their widely different individual preferences.

This essay has been about Christian values in relation to the market. Yet the importance of values applies to all aspects of our society. The one issue which remains is the source of such values. Hayek freely admits that a free society in itself is no guarantee that it can generate those values which are necessary to its survival. The one institution which more than any other should be the keeper of those values is the church. Events in Eastern Europe have shown just how great a power the church has to influence politics, when it remains true to these values. Religion alone provides meaning to our lives. Christian values in this type of a society are a strong basis for both freedom and prosperity. In terms of responsible wealth creation, the building of communities, creating public/private partnerships to deal with inner city regeneration, developing the potential of children in school through what is taught to them, the churches have enormous opportunities to realize their values in action. But the question remains whether our spiritual leaders still have the will to proclaim them.

# Notes

### The shaping of a Christian's approach to politics

1 W. Jordan, *The State: Authority and Autonomy* (Blackwell, 1985).

### Towards a Christian view of state and economy

1 See A. Wolters, *Creation Regained* (IVP, 1986); B. Walsh and R. Middleton, *The Transforming Vision* (Downer's Grove: IVP, 1984); *Worldviews and Social Science*, eds. P. Marshall, R. Mouw, and S. Griffioen (University Press of America, 1987).

2 See B. Goudzwaard, *Capitalism and Progress* (Eerdmans, 1979).

3 J. M. Keynes, *The General Theory of Employment, Interest and Money* (Macmillan, 1936), p. 383.

4 I say 'a suggested Christian policy' not because I believe there may be several Christian economic policies (though I am open to the view that there are) but because I have no wish to suggest that mine is the final word.

5 *Cf.* E. Brunner, *Justice and the Social Order* (Lutterworth, 1945), p. 89. See also P. Marshall, *Human Rights Theories in Christian Perspective* (Toronto: Institute for Christian Studies, 1983), pp. 17–23; and B. Zylstra, 'The Bible, Justice and the State', *International Reformed Bulletin*, 55 (1973), pp. 2–18.

6 The following discussion is based on P. Marshall, 'Justice for the Poor', *Political Service Bulletin* of Citizens for Public Justice, Toronto (August, 1980).

7 This expression was coined by H. E. Runner. Its implications are sketched out in *Life is Religion*, ed. H. Vander Goot (Paideia Press, 1981), which was a *Festschrift* dedicated to Runner.

8  The theme of idolatry in relation to the family is explored in J. A. Walter, *A Long Way from Home: A Sociological Exploration of Contemporary Idolatry* (Paternoster Press, 1980).

9  B. Goudzwaard, *Aid for the Overdeveloped West* (Wedge, 1975), pp. 14–15. Goudzwaard develops the meaning of idolatry and discusses the modern idols of 'nation', 'revolution', 'material prosperity' and 'guaranteed security' in *Idols of Our Time* (Downers Grove: IVP, 1984).

10  J. K. Galbraith, *The New Industrial State* (Penguin, 1968), p. 162.

11  J. M. Keynes, *Essays in Persuasion* (Macmillan, 1972), p. 331.

12  This understanding of government policy as a 'two-track' approach was formulated by Stanley Carlson-Thies in *Groping Towards an Understanding of the Roles of Canadian Governments in Promoting and Distorting Wellbeing* (Toronto: Citizens for Public Justice, 1977).

## A Labour Party view

1  *Meet the Challenge, Make the Change* (Labour Party, 1989).

2  This definition begs the question, raised by Karl Marx and others, whether ideology is merely a tool for the distortion of reality by abstraction.

3  *E.g.* J. L. Segundo, *The Liberation of Theology* (Orbis, 1976).

4  For a popular account, see M. and R. Friedman, *Free to Choose* (Pelican, 1980).

5  See C. B. Macpherson, *The Political Theory of Possessive Individualism* (Oxford University Press, 1962).

6  *E.g.* the body of Christ metaphor (1 Cor. 12), and Paul's speech to the city council at Athens (Acts 17:16–31).

7  See B. Griffiths, *Morality and the Market Place* (Hodder and Stoughton, 1982).

8  See the Church of England Board for Social Responsibility's report, *Not Just for the Poor* (Church House Publishing, 1986).

9  'A fairer community: economic activity' in *Meet the Challenge, Make the Change*.

10  See the thesis propounded in M. Weber, *The Protestant Ethic and the Spirit of Capitalism* (Allen and Unwin, 1977).

11  For a Christian exposition of the issues surrounding this proposition, see R. Preston, *The Future of Christian Ethics* (SCM, 1987), pp. 130 ff.

12  'A better quality of life' in *Meet the Challenge, Make the Change*.

13 *North-South: A Programme for Survival* (Pan, 1980).
14 E.g. B. Griffiths, *Morality and the Market Place*.
15 J. Stott, *Issues Facing Christians Today* (Marshalls, 1984), pp. 128–134.
16 See J. A. Walter, *A Long Way from Home: A Sociological Exploration of Contemporary Idolatry* (Paternoster Press, 1980).
17 *Not Just for the Poor*, pp. 119–132.
18 'A commitment to excellence' in *Meet the Challenge, Make the Change*.
19 *Not Just for the Poor*, pp. 87–91, and Friedman, *Free to Choose*, pp. 118–158.
20 The government 'needs assessment' figures are virtually meaningless to the average citizen, and are not based on genuinely objective criteria, but rather on politically motivated gerrymandering of the figures.
21 W. Temple, *Christianity and Social Order* (Penguin, 1942), pp. 64–69.
22 See Preston, *The Future of Christian Ethics*, pp. 204–219.
23 P. Hinchliff, *Holiness and Politics* (Darton, Longman and Todd, 1982), p. 194.
24 Preston, *The Future of Christian Ethics*, p. 213.
25 Based on a talk given by Brian Griffiths at a consultation on Christianity and the New Right.
26 See K. Mannheim, *Ideology and Utopia* (Routledge and Kegan Paul, 1936).
27 I recall suggesting this at a seminar on Christianity and politics, to be met with the response that if God had meant us to worry about political values, he would have made it clear in Scripture! – a response that begs so many questions that one hardly knew where to start.
28 Preston, *The Future of Christian Ethics*, p. 135.
29 J. Rawls, *A Theory of Justice* (Harvard, 1971).
30 There is no grammatical distinction between 'freedom' and 'liberty'. They are here taken to express the same concept.
31 Lord Harris, 'The Morality of the Market' in *The New Right and Christian Values* (Centre for Theology and Public Issues, 1987), p. 13.

**Biblical theology and the politics of the Centre**

1 See J. Goldingay, *Approaches to Old Testament Interpretation* (IVP, 1981), pp. 38–43, 51–61; C. J. Wright, *Living as the*

*People of God* (IVP, 1983); O. M. O'Donovan, 'The Possibility of a Biblical Ethic', *TST Bulletin*, 67 (1973), pp. 15–23; T. W. Ogletree, *The Use of the Bible in Christian Ethics* (Blackwell, 1983).

2 D. Steel, 'Liberalism', *A New Dictionary of Christian Ethics*, eds. J. Macquarrie and J. Childress (SCM, 1986), pp. 347–349. See also J. P. Wogaman, *Christian Perspectives on Politics* (SCM, 1988), ch. 6; G. Sabine, *A History of Political Theory* (Harrap, 1963), chs. 31 and 32.

3 See M. Thatcher, *Let Our Children Grow Tall* (Centre for Policy Studies, 1977).

4 See I. Berlin, 'Two Concepts of Liberty' in M. Sandel, *Liberalism and Its Critics* (Blackwell, 1984), pp. 16–36.

5 See F. Hayek, *The Constitution of Liberty* (Routledge & Kegan Paul, 1962); F. Hayek, *Law, Legislation and Liberty* (Routledge & Kegan Paul, 1973); K. Joseph and J. Sumption, *Equality* (Murray, 1977).

6 See R. Plant, 'Challenges to Conservative Capitalism' in A. Harvey, *Theology in the City* (SPCK, 1989), ch. 4.

7 See R. Bauckham, *The Bible in Politics* (SPCK, 1989), p. 105.

8 See J. Blunck, 'Freedom' in *A New International Dictionary of New Testament Theology*, vol. I, ed. C. Brown (Paternoster Press, 1975), pp. 715–720.

9 Bauckham, *The Bible in Politics*, p. 106.

10 Bauckham, *The Bible in Politics*, p. 106.

11 See Wright, *Living as the People of God*, ch. 3; W. Brueggeman, *The Land* (Fortress Press, 1977).

12 See H. Thielicke, *Theological Ethics: Politics* (Eerdmans, 1979), part 2.

13 Bauckham, *The Bible in Politics*, p. 107.

14 See Sabine, *A History of Political Theory*, chs. 31 and 32.

15 Sandel, *Liberalism and Its Critics*, p. 9.

16 D. Owen, *Face the Future* (Oxford University Press, 1981), p. 3.

17 John Atherton in ch. 2 of his book *Faith in the Nation* (SPCK, 1988), speaks of 'corporate images'. The term 'motif' seems to me, however, to be less misleading.

18 For a review of literature on the image of God, see Ray S. Anderson, *On Being Human* (Eerdmans, 1982), ch. 6 and Appendix B; Douglas Hall, *Imaging God* (Eerdmans, 1986), chs. 2, 3.

19 On the importance of covenant see Wright, *Living as the People of God*, esp. pp. 63–64.

20 See Bauckham, *The Bible in Politics*, pp. 106–109; Wright, *Living as the People of God*, ch. 6.

21 Atherton, *Faith in the Nation*, pp. 26 ff.

22 Atherton, *Faith in the Nation*, p. 28.

23 See Paul S. Minnear, *Images of the Church in the New Testament* (Westminster Press, 1960), ch. IV.

24 See G. E. Ladd, *The Presence of the Future* (SPCK, 1980); Stephen Travis, *I Believe in the Second Coming of Jesus* (Hodder and Stoughton 1982), ch. 2; J. Moltmann, *The Trinity and the Kingdom of God* (SCM, 1981).

25 See N. Cohn, *The Pursuit of the Millennium* (Paladin, 1970).

26 See Bauckham, *The Bible in Politics*, ch. 3; David Atkinson, *Pastoral Ethics in Practice* (Monarch, 1989), ch. 7, esp. pp. 136 ff.

27 Kenneth Leech, *True God* (Sheldon Press, 1985), p. 245. It should perhaps be stressed here that Leech does not seek to argue that the face of Christ should be seen in the Hitlers and Stalins of this world but rather that the incarnation reminds us that the fact of humanity must be taken seriously.

28 Leonardo Boff, *Trinity and Society* (Burns and Oates, 1988), pp. 127–28.

29 Boff, *Trinity and Society*, pp. 15–16.

30 Boff, *Trinity and Society*, p. 11.

31 Boff, *Trinity and Society*, p. 16.

32 Boff, *Trinity and Society*, pp. 150–51.

## A Conservative view of the policy of full employment

1 The word translated here 'ten-acre' is in Hebrew 'ten-yoke', i.e. the land ploughed by ten yoke of oxen in one day. A 'bath' was approximately 5 gallons or 22 litres; a 'homer' 220 litres and an 'epah' 22 litres.

## Response by Francis Bridger

1 C. J. Wright, *Living as the People of God* (IVP, 1983).

2 O. M. O'Donovan, *Resurrection and Moral Order* (IVP, 1986).

## Economic policy and the Welfare State

1 B. Griffiths, *The Creation of Wealth* (Hodder and Stoughton, 1984), pp. 18–23.

2 I. Kirzner, *Prime Mover of Progress: The Entrepreneur in Capitalism and Socialism* (Institute of Economic Affairs, 1980).

3 See S. Hall and M. Jacques, *The Politics of Thatcherism* (Lawrence and Wishart, 1983), and *New Times: The Changing Face of Politics in the 1990s*, eds. S. Hall and M. Jacques (Lawrence and Wishart, 1989).

4 D. Turner and C. Williams, *An Investment Bank for the UK* (Fabian, 1987).

5 R. Hattersley, *Economic Priorities for a Labour Government* (Macmillan, 1987).

6 R. Skidelsky, *The Social Market Economy* (Social Market Foundation, 1989).

## The political parties and biblical principles

1 The evolution of the Conservative position can be seen in the following 'election specials': Lord Hailsham, *The Conservative Case* (Penguin, 1959); T. Raison, *Why Conservative?* (Penguin, 1964); C. Patten, *The Tory Case* (Longman, 1983). The 'neo-liberal' position is illustrated in Sir Keith Joseph, *Reversing the Trend* (Centre for Policy Studies, 1975); M. Thatcher, *Let Our Children Grow Tall* (Centre for Policy Studies, 1977). The 'traditionalist critique' is illustrated in Sir Ian Gilmour, *Inside Right* (Hutchinson, 1977); F. Pym, *The Politics of Consent* (Constable, 1985).

2 The different emphases can be seen in the revisionist classic, C. A. R. Crosland, *The Future of Socialism* (Cape, 1956) which contrasts with A. W. Benn, *Arguments for Socialism* (Cape, 1979) and *Arguments for Democracy* (Cape, 1981). R. Hattersley, *Choose Freedom* (Michael Joseph, 1987) is a contemporary restatement of the case for democratic socialism. N. Kinnock, *Making Our Way* (Blackwells, 1986) sets out the philosophy and policies of the current leadership.

3 SDP thinking was set out in D. Owen, *Face the Future* (Cape, 1981). The Alliance position was fully articulated in D. Steel and D. Owen, *The Time Has Come* (Weidenfeld and Nicolson, 1987).

## Appendix

1 In *Christianity and Conservatism: Are Christianity and Conservatism Compatible?*, eds. M. Alison and D. Edwards (Hodder and Stoughton, 1990).

# About the contributors

**Jonathan Chaplin**, editor of this volume, is tutor in politics, Plater College, Oxford.

**Francis Bridger** is a Liberal Democratic councillor on Broxtowe Borough Council, Vicar of Woodthorpe, and associate lecturer in philosophy at St John's College, Nottingham.

**Pete Broadbent** is Vicar of Trinity St Michael, Harrow. He was, for seven years, a Labour councillor in the London Borough of Islington. Some of the material in his contribution has previously appeared in *Third Way*.

**Sir Fred Catherwood** is a Vice-President of the European Parliament and author of *Pro-Europe?* (IVP, 1991). He has been MEP for Cambridgeshire for twelve years.

**Philip Giddings** is lecturer in politics at the University of Reading, and member of the General Synod of the Church of England.

**Lord Griffiths of Fforestfach** is an adviser and banker. He is adviser to Goldman Sachs and Chairman of the School Examination and Assessment Council.

**Paul Marshall** comes from Liverpool, studied at Manchester University, and is senior member in political theory at the Institute for Christian Studies in Toronto. He is author of *Thine is the Kingdom: A Biblical Perspective on Politics Today*, and several other books.

**Donald Shell** is lecturer in politics at the University of Bristol, and author of *The House of Lords* (Simon and Schuster, second edition, 1992). He is preparing a companion volume on the House of Commons.

**Alan Storkey** is a social scientist lecturing at Oak Hill College, where he co-ordinates Pastoral Studies. He helped to form the Movement for Christian Democracy, and is author of several books.

# About the contributors

**Oliver R. Barclay**, the editor of the *When Christians Disagree* series, was formerly General Secretary of the Universities and Colleges Christian Fellowship. He has written on social-ethical issues, and encouraged Christian involvement in politics over many years.